How the Heck Did They Get Those Names?

Ron Tavernit

Copyright © 2024 Ron Tavernit
All rights reserved
First Edition

PAGE PUBLISHING
Conneaut Lake, PA

First originally published by Page Publishing 2024

ISBN 979-8-89157-964-4 (pbk)
ISBN 979-8-89157-993-4 (digital)

Printed in the United States of America

I would like to dedicate this book to my wonderful wife, Carol, and to all five of our incredible kids and fantastic grandkids. They were all enthusiastic. My wife has encouraged me from day one. When I stopped working on the book at various times, she would ask if I did anything more on it and when was I getting back to it? Honestly, I had a difficult time getting back to it from time to time, but she kept mentioning it. I also had some very good friends who encouraged me like my buddy Big Al Muscovitz, who was a great radio friend and now writes for the Jewish News in Michigan. And then there was a high school friend who I sat next to recently at a small reunion dinner. I mentioned the book (that was just about finished), and she was very encouraging and inspiring and insisted I get it going. Thank you, Charlene Kavanagh Tocco. A week after speaking to you I called the good folks at Page Publishing and got the ball rolling. Thank you to all.

PREFACE

Information in this book was gathered in many different ways.

First and foremost by conversations I had with numerous other radio personalities' program directors and other individuals in the radio industry, many of whom had firsthand knowledge from a variety of artists and groups they featured on their radio shows.

Information I obtained during interviews I personally had with a variety of singers and band members.

Information I obtained by research from a variety of sources. They include the following:

- *The Rolling Stone Encyclopedia of Rock & Roll*, edited by Jon Pareles and Patricia Romanowski
- *Rock On* by Norm N. Nite with Ralph M. Newman
- *That Old Time Rock & Roll* by Richard Aquila
- *Top 40 Hits* by Joel Whitburn
- Wikipedia
- Websites of groups and singers

Thank you for your understanding.

INTRODUCTION

If you grew up listening to rock and roll music from the fifties, sixties, and seventies, you might be interested to know how groups and singers from that era got their names—groups like the Beatles, Rolling Stones, and Three Dog Night, and singers like Chubby Checker and Conway Twitty, along with so many others. When I played their music, I became intrigued with how and why they selected those names and if it was actually them that picked them (interestingly in many cases, it was not). As it was, I talked to a number of other DJs and people in the industry who knew some of the stories behind those names.

After retiring from the business in 2008, I started researching the topic. I have several books in my possession that encompass the stories of many of them. I also did a mountain of research on the web, including websites of singers and groups as well as Wikipedia and so many other sites. The more research I did, the more interesting it became. It was at that point that I thought a book might be the way to go.

Included in the book are little tidbits of disc jockey humor that I hope you might like. I have also included some names you might not recognize just because I found their stories interesting.

Thank you, and please enjoy!

10CC

Caution: Younger readers should avoid this one!

Original members that each played several instruments
- Graham Gouldman
- Eric Stewart
- Kevin Godley
- Lol Cream

10cc is an English rock band whose greatest success came in the seventies. One of their greatest distinctions (in my opinion) is that every member played a variety of instruments. The group had many personnel changes over the years.

10cc actually started as a three-man group known as the Hotlegs. The story regarding the new name of the band was that Jonathan King, the group's producer, had a dream where he saw a header in London reading "10cc the Best Band in the World." At this point, some members of the band suggested 10cc might represent something else. (Younger readers might want to consider parental permission to read further.)

What 10cc might represent (according to some members of the band) is the large amount of semen ejaculated by a rather proficient man during a sexual encounter. That story is disputed by some but confirmed by others directly associated with the band. Just to be accurate (I do have occasional notions of accuracy), the actual amount during such an encounter is said to be closer to 3 cc. (I wonder who decided to do the measuring!) Now, even though I have done some rather proud measuring in my life, I've never measured that.

Also see Lovin' Spoonful' (yep, you guessed it, same kind of thing).

My favorite 10cc songs
- '76: "The Things We Do for Love"
- '77: "People in Love

1910 FRUITGUM COMPANY

Original members
    Frank Jeckell
    Mark Gutkowski
    Floyd Marcus
    Pat Karwan
    Steve Mortkowitz

This band started with an interesting name, Jeckell and the Hydes, from New Jersey. In the late sixties, record producers Jerry Kasenetz and Jeff Katz felt the subteen market had not yet been tapped, so they found Jeckell and the Hydes and called their efforts bubblegum music. One of the producers then found an old gum wrapper on the sidewalk with a name on it and suggested the group use that as their name—1910 Fruitgum Company was born. (Gee! Bubblegum music! Makes sense.)

Interesting note: The group really didn't do any of the vocals on their recordings. (Whaaat!) That was saved for a number of studio musicians and lead singer Joey Levine (not a member of the group). Their biggest hit was from 1968 called "Simon Says."

My favorite 1910 Fruitgum Company song
    '68: "Simon Says" (go figure)

ABBA

Original members
    Agnetha Faitskog
    Bjorn Ulvaeus
    Benny Andersson
    Anni-Frida Lyngstad

ABBA formed in Sweden in 1972 and quickly became one of the most successful groups in history. The group's name is taken from the first letters in the group's first names, *A*gnetha Faitskog, *B*jorn Ulvaeus, *B*enny Andersson, and *A*nni-Frida Lyngstad.

Prior to 1972, all four of the members had somewhat successful careers in the performing arts in Sweden. Benny was a member of a group called the Hep Stars, Bjorn was with the Hootenanny Singers, Anna was a popular female vocalist, and Frida was featured on a TV program called *Hyland's Corner*.

Agnetha and Bjorn were a married couple, as were Benny and Anni-Frida. Unfortunately, the success of the group also took a toll and led to the demise of their marriages. It is said (I heard this from several sources) that even though they achieved great success in English-speaking countries like the US and UK, they did not speak a word of the language. They simply learned the phonetic pronunciations of their songs before performing.

My favorite ABBA songs
    '74: "Waterloo"
    '76: "Mamma Mia"
    '76: "Dancing Queen"
    '76: "Fernando"
    '78: "Take a Chance on Me"

AEROSMITH

Original members
  Steve Tyler, vocals, keyboards
  Joe Perry, guitar
  Tom Hamilton, bass
  Joey Kramer, drums

Joe Perry and Tom Hamilton started as the Jam Band and played an event with Chain Reaction, a group that Steve Tyler started. In 1970, the groups got together to consider joining as one. From that point, they began putting songs together and rehearsing together.

The next job was to agree on a name, and there are a number of stories about that. The first is they spent a lot of time smoking pot and watching old Three Stooges episodes (well, who among us hasn't done that!), and at one of these sessions, they came up with the name Aerosmith. Another is that one of the members said he wrote the word *Aerosmith* on his books in high school. He said it came from a Harry Nilsson album called *Aerial Ballet*. The group also considered the names the Hookers and Spike Jones. (Hookers would have been an interesting choice, but I think Tyler would have needed even more serious makeup and maybe a mini skirt. Now try to get that image out of your head.)

Aerosmith has sold more than 150 million records and is widely known as the greatest American hard rock band of all time. They were credited with numerous awards, including being inducted into the Rock and Roll Hall of Fame in 2001.

My favorite Aerosmith songs
  '73: "Dream On"
  '75: "Walk This Way"

ALICE COOPER

Original members
Vince Furnier, lead singer
Glen Buxton, lead guitar
Michael, rhythm guitar, keyboards
Dennis Dunaway, bass
Neal Smith, drums

Vincent Damon Furnier was born in Detroit in 1948. In 1964, after moving to Arizona, Furnier got a group of guys together from his high school track team to perform at the school's talent show. They were originally known as the Earwigs, followed by the Spiders and the Nazz. After they realized that Todd Rundgren's band was also known as Nazz, they figured they needed another name change.

The story goes that their name came about from a Ouija board that indicated Alice Cooper was a witch from the 1600s. Furnier decided a gimmick like that might work, especially since their music was somewhat on the extreme side of psychedelic rock. Furnier also decided that wearing outrageous women's clothing would give them the look they wanted (hmmm, maybe he just liked that look). Just a note here: Alice Cooper was the band's name, not Furnier's—at least for a while.

One night, the band played at a club and within a few minutes cleared the place out with their bombastic style (the club must have loved that). However, producer Shep Gordon saw the performance and thought, in the right circumstance, it could work. He introduced the group to Frank Zappa, who took them under his wing. The group traveled to California, where they thought they could make it big. However, they were not well received there. Furnier claims Californians were just on the wrong drugs (I hate when that happens). They were, however, well received in Pontiac, Michigan, close to Furnier's home in Detroit. (I guess we had better drugs... or worse.)

One of the biggest events for Alice Cooper came when a live chicken crossed the stage in the middle of a performance in Toronto. Furnier claims he thought the chicken could fly, so he picked it up and threw it into the crowd. Apparently, members of the crowd (some say, who were in wheelchairs) tore the chicken apart (gee, that sounds like fun, maybe Toronto had the best drugs of all). When the press got ahold of the story, they claimed Furnier actually bit the head off the chicken and drank the blood. Furnier says he never did that, but Zappa liked the connotation and encouraged him to not dispute the story. Alice Cooper then became known for the shock rock style. Furnier also decided to take the name Alice Cooper for himself.

My favorite Alice Cooper song
    '71: "School's Out"

AMERICA

Original members
  Dewey Bunnell
  Dan Peek
  Gerry Beckley

Despite the name America, this group first got together in London, England. All three members were the sons of American servicemen stationed in the UK at an air force base. Hence the reason they took the name America. It is also said they did not want people to think they were an English band trying to sound American.

My favorite America songs
  '72: "A Horse with No Name"
  '72: "Ventura Highway"
  '75: "Sister Golden Hair"

AMERICAN BREED

Original members
>Gary Loizzo, vocals, guitar
>Charles Colbert Jr., bass, vocals
>Al Ciner, guitar, vocals
>Jim Michalak, drums

American Breed was formed in Illinois with lead singer Gary Loizzo along with Charles Colbert, Al Ciner, and Lee Graziano, under the name Gary & the Knight Lites. "Bend Me, Shape Me" was their biggest hit, reaching number 5 on Billboard in 1968.

The band name came about when they were first signed to a record deal but were told their name sounded "a little dated." According to Loizzo, they threw some names in a hat and picked out American Breed.

My favorite American Breed song
>'67: "Bend Me, Shape Me"

THE ANIMALS

Original members
    Eric Burden, vocals
    Hilton Valentine, lead guitar
    Alan Price, keyboard
    Bryan "Chas" Chandler, bass
    John Steel, drums

This group formed in Newcastle upon Tyne, England (that's a hell of a name for a town), in 1958 as the Alan Price Combo and became very popular in England. It is said their name, the Animals, came because of their wild appearance (especially that of lead singer Eric Burdon). However, Burdon says that wasn't true, and that the name was a tribute to a friend of the group named Animal Hogg. (Now there's a name for a résumé. Maybe he could work at a zoo!)

The Animals were inducted into the Rock and Roll Hall of Fame in 1994.

My favorite Animals songs
    '64: "House of the Rising Sun"
    '65: "We Gotta Get Out of this Place"
    '65: "Don't Let Me Be Misunderstood"
    '66: "Don't Bring Me Down"
    '66: "See See Rider"

ARCHIES

Original members (cartoon characters)
- Archie
- Reggie
- Jughead
- Veronica
- Betty

This band was purely fictional. They did have a number 1 pop hit in 1969 called "Sugar Sugar," but again, they were fictional. How did that happen? Well, the group was part of an animated TV series called "The Archie Show." Its members were Archie, Reggie, Jughead, Veronica, and Betty. Now if you remember the *Archie* comic book series, that should ring a bell (I was a big fan, and those original comic books are probably worth a bunch now—damn, I tossed them out). The group was also part of the bubblegum pop genre. The Archies featured another song called "Jingle Jangle," whose female vocals were said to have been sung by Betty and Veronica but were actually sung by Ron Dante in a falsetto style.

The Archies' music was actually performed by a bunch of studio musicians and included Ron Dante on lead vocals. Dante was also known for recording another hit song called "Tracy" by the Cuff Links. As a matter of fact, Dante *was* the Cuff Links. He recorded all the voices and overdubbed each one with the harmonic lines. What's really bizarre is that at the same time "Sugar Sugar" was on the national charts, "Tracy" was in the process of becoming a hit for the Cuff Links.

But that's not all! Dante also sang lead for another bubblebum group called the Detergents, who hit with "Leader of the Laundromat." That song was a parody of a song from the Shangri-Las called "Leader of the Pack." Ron Dante was a very busy guy and knew how to operate a multitrack tape recorder.

My favorite Archies, Cufflinks, and Detergents (Ron Dante) songs
'69: "Sugar Sugar"
'69: "Tracy"
'65: "Leader of the Laundromat"

B.B. King

Riley B. King was born in Itta Bena, Mississippi, in 1925. Itta Bena was in the cotton country, so in his early years he picked cotton for around thirty-five cents per one hundred pounds. Later, King taught himself to play the guitar and listened to a number of blues artists on the radio. At one point, he worked at radio station WDIA in Memphis, Tennessee, and was given the nickname Beale Street Blues Boy. That name later became just Beale Boy, which was eventually shortened to B B, and the name B.B. King was born.

B.B. King was well-known for performing an incredible number of shows every year sometimes, topping two hundred concerts through age seventy. King was inducted into the Blues Hall of Fame in 1980 and the Rock and Roll Hall of Fame in 1987 and was given the nickname the King of the Blues. King was apparently prolific in another area. He is said to have fifteen children with fifteen different mothers. (No wonder he performed so many shows. He had to feed a lot of people.)

There is also an interesting story about King and his guitar. In 1949, King was performing at a dance hall in the town of Twist, Arkansas. At some point, two men got into a fight and knocked over a barrel of kerosene. The building caught on fire and sent everybody running, including King. B.B. then realized he left his guitar inside and ran back in to get it. Later, King learned that the two men were fighting over a woman named Lucille. At that point, King named his guitar Lucille and did the same with every guitar he owned after that. He also vowed to never do something as stupid as running into a burning building no matter what was there.

King also memorialized the incident by writing and recording the song "Lucille," which became a huge hit.

Gibson guitars (the maker of most of King's instruments) made eighty special Lucille guitars in 2005 for King's eightieth birthday and gave the first one to King. Some years later, the guitar was stolen. It was found to be purchased from a Las Vegas pawnshop and was returned to King in 2009. King died in 2015 at age eighty-nine.

My favorite B.B. King songs
　　'68: "Lucille"
　　'69: "The Thrill Is Gone"

BACHMAN-TURNER OVERDRIVE

Original members
  Randy Bachman, guitar, lead vocals
  Fred Turner, bass, vocals
  Tim Bachman, guitar, vocals
  Blair Thornton replaced Tim
  Robbie Bachman, drums

BTO, as it's sometimes called, had their roots in Winnipeg, Manitoba, Canada. Members first played under the name Chad Allen and the Expressions. After Allen decided to leave, Randy Bachman reorganized the group into the Guess Who, one of Canada's most influential rock bands.

Randy then left the Guess Who for a solo career in 1970 but soon after got back together with his brothers (Robby and Tim Bachman) and Chad Allen (again) to form Brave Belt. Allen (again) left the group and was replaced by Fred Turner, and they reformed as Bachman-Turner Overdrive.

While on the way back from Toronto after playing a gig and while the group was still called Brave Belt, they had dinner at a steak house in Windsor, Ontario. There they spotted a trucker magazine called *Overdrive*. That part of the name clicked, so the *Overdrive* portion of their new name came from, of all things, the magazine *Overdrive* and the rest from its members.

See "The Guess Who." That's a very interesting story too.

My favorite BTO songs
  '74: "Let It Ride"
  '74: "Takin' Care of Business"
  '74: "You Ain't Seen Nothing Yet"
  '75: "Roll on Down the Highway"

Bay City Rollers

Original members
    Eric Faulkner, guitar
    Stuart Wood, guitar
    Less McKeown, vocals
    Alan Longmuir, bass
    Derek Longmuir, drums

I always thought these guys were from Bay City, Michigan. Actually there are a couple of connections to Michigan for this group. The Bay City Rollers formed in the late sixties and were one of the most successful groups to come out of Scotland! Edinburgh, Scotland, to be exact. While Edinburgh is on the coast of the North Sea in Scotland, there's no town nearby called Bay City.

Originally the group was a trio consisting of Alan Longmuir, his brother Derek, and Neil Porteous called the Ambassadors. Soon after, they made some adjustments and became the Saxons and did very well in Scotland and England.

The group enjoyed performing Motown songs but especially liked a song called "C.C. Rider" by Mitch Rider and the Detroit Wheels (I always love it when there's a Detroit connection). The group also decided they needed a new name, something that was more American sounding, before trying to make it in the US. It is said that their manager, Tam Paton, threw a dart onto a map of the United States. And where did it land? Arkansas! Little Rock Rollers just didn't have a good ring to it, so he tried again, and you got it—Bay City, Michigan—and from that day forward they were to be known as the Bay City Rollers. Thank goodness he didn't hit Flint or Toledo. It just wouldn't have had the same ring to it.

My favorite Bay City Rollers songs
    '75: "Saturday Night"
    '76: "Money Honey"
    '76: "I Only Wanna Be with You"
    '77: "The Way I Feel Tonight"

BEACH BOYS

Brian Wilson
Dennis Wilson
Carl Wilson
Mike Love
Al Jardine

This group is credited with introducing the California surf sound to America. Brothers Brian, Dennis, and Carl Wilson along with their cousin Mike Love and good friend Al Jardine started the group. Love actually gave the group their first name the Pendletones after a popular shirt of the time.

Dennis Wilson suggested they consider singing about his favorite sport, surfing. (Interestingly, Dennis was the only one of the group that actually surfed at the time.) Brian Wilson then wrote the song "Surfin." The brothers' dad, Murry Wilson, who was an accomplished piano player and songwriter of the time, arranged for his publisher to meet the Pendletones. Murray admits he didn't like the song at all, but still arranged the meeting with the group and publisher Hite Morgan.

Morgan and his wife heard the "Surfin" song, and it was Mrs. Morgan who said "Drop everything, we're going to record your song. I think it's good." The rest, as they say, is history; except for one little detail. The boys recorded the song on September 15, 1961, and then rerecorded it at a major studio in Hollywood on October 3. Herb Newman, a record company owner, then signed the group to a contract with Candix Records. The single was released some weeks later, and it was at this time they found out they had been renamed from the Pendletones to the Beach Boys. (That would be like changing my name from Ron to Butch without me knowing!) The song was a regional hit, but because Candix couldn't keep up with back orders for the song, they went bankrupt. Soon after, the Beach Boys signed with Capitol Records.

Quick personal story about the Beach Boy hit "Barbara Ann." I interviewed Dean Torrance of Jan and Dean back at a festival one summer in Novi, Michigan. Dean said that he sang with the Beach Boys on one particular recording of their song "Barbara Ann." Well, after the interview, I was to emcee a show they (Jan and Dean) were doing later that evening. At the show, I introduced them and knew that, after their performance, they would be coming back for an encore. As they were coming back up on stage and I was walking off, Dean grabbed my arm and said to come on back. They had me sing with them the song "Barbara Ann." What a great experience!

My favorite Beach Boys songs
'61: "Surfin"
'62: "Surfin' Safari"
'62: "409"
'63: "Surfin' USA"
'63: "Surfer Girl"
'63: "Be True to Your School"
'63: "Shut Down"
'63: "Little Deuce Coupe"
'63: "In My Room"
'64: "Little Honda"
'64: "I Get Around"
'65: "Barbara Ann" (especially with my help)
'65: "California Girls"
'65: "Help Me, Rhonda"
'66: "Good Vibrations"
'66: "Wouldn't It Be Nice"
'82: "California Dreamin'"

BEATLES

Original members
    John Lennon, vocals, guitar
    Paul McCartney, vocals, guitar
    George Harrison, vocals, bass
    Stu Sutcliff, guitar, left the group to pursue an art career
    Tommy Moore, drummer, replaced by Pete Best, who was replaced in 1962 by Ringo Starr, drummer, vocals

The Beatles (John Lennon and Paul McCartney) began as a skiffle group called the Blackjacks, whose name quickly changed to the Quarrymen in 1957 because John was going to Quarry Bank High School in Liverpool and because there was another group known as the Blackjacks. (Skiffle was a music genre that included jazz, blues, and American folk and became popular in England in the 1950s.) Soon after that, George Harrison joined the group, and they changed their name to Johnny and the Moondogs. Stu Sutcliff (bass player) and Tommy Moore (drummer) also joined in 1959, and they changed their name again to the Silver Beatles. Pete Best then replaced Moore. Sutcliff then left the group to concentrate on his art (he was a fine painter at the time).

It was about that same time that the Silver Beatles were heard on a recording for the first time. Actually for this song, they revised their name to the Beat Brothers. They were the backup band for a famous European singer by the name of Tony Sheridan. The song was "My Bonnie," an old Scottish folk song believed to have originated in the late 1700s. Many readers who are somewhat advanced in age (including me) remember the song's lyrics that begin with "My Bonnie lies over the ocean, my Bonnie lies over the sea." There's an old 45 record out there (first time Beatles are heard on a recording) somewhere in the archives (unfortunately not in my archives) that might be worth a considerable sum.

That brings us to 1962, when Pete Best (the group's self-proclaimed stud muffin) was asked to leave the band to be replaced by

Ringo Starr (great drummer but definitely not a stud muffin). And there you have the four names we are all so familiar with: John, Paul, George, and Ringo. By now, they dropped Silver from their name and would be called the Beatles from that day forward.

It is said that Stu Sutcliff originally suggested the name as a tribute to Buddy Holly and the Crickets. The Beatles were big fans of Holly's music and must have had a thing for bugs as well. Years later, Paul McCartney actually purchased the rights to all of Holly's music.

My favorite Beatles songs
    All of them!

BEAU BRUMMELS

Original members
    Sal Valentino, vocals
    Ron Elliott, guitar
    Ron Meagher, bass
    Declan Mulligan, guitar, bass, harmonica
    John Petersen, drums

This group was formed in 1964 in San Francisco by Sal Valentino and Ron Elliott. While performing at a local club, they ran into Tom Donahue, who was trying to form a record label. Donahue took them on along with another guy, Sylvester Stewart, who would later become Sly Stewart of Sly and the Family Stone. He helped the group record a huge hit in 1965 called "Laugh Laugh."

The song was no laughing matter, and a little-known fact about it is that "Laugh Laugh" is considered by the Rock and Roll Hall of Fame as one of the five hundred songs that shaped rock and roll!

The name Beau Brummels apparently comes from the fact that it was British sounding, which worked out nice since it was at the height of the British Invasion, and that alphabetically Beau Brummels would follow Beatles in record bins across the country. In an interview with *Goldmine* magazine, Sal Valentino says no way, "that's a total myth" and "We just needed a name and that sounded good" (oh yeah, Beau Brummels, that's a name that would immediately come to mind).

My favorite Beau Brummels songs
    '65: "Laugh Laugh"
    '65: "Just a Little"

BEE GEES

Original members
  Barry Gibb
  Robin Gibb
  Maurice Gibb

This group from the town of Douglas on the Isle of Mann (an island in the Irish Sea between England and Ireland) consisted of three members. They were all brothers, two of which were twins (Robin and Maurice). Barry was about two years older. They first performed, as youngsters, calling themselves the Rattlesnakes and the Bluecats. In the late fifties, the family moved to Australia, where the group performed at local clubs. Then they decided to change their name and became the Bee Gees for Brothers Gibb.

There is, however, some dispute over that. In about 1960, the younger twins (Barry and Robin) performed at a race track near Brisbane at the request of a driver there by the name Bill Goode. The boys would ride in the back of a truck and sing while patrons would throw money at them that they were able to keep. Goode is said to have named the group BGs for Barry's initials and his. (The Brothers Gibb story sounds good, but the other is, I think, plausible.)

The Bee Gees were very popular in Australia and even had their own TV show. They moved back to the UK, and the rest is history. The Bee Gees have sold over two hundred million records, including their biggest success, the album *Saturday Night Fever*, from the movie, selling more than fifteen million LPs. Maurice died in 2003, and Robin and Barry then retired the name. A few years later, they decided to restore the name and perform again. However, Robin then died in 2012.

My favorite Bee Gees songs
  '67: "New York Mining Disaster, 1941"
  '67: "To Love Somebody"
  '67: "Massachusetts"

'68: "I've Got a Message for You"
'68: "I Started a Joke"
'70: "Lonely Days"
'77: "How Deep Is Your Love"
'77: "Stayin' Alive"
'78: "Night Fever"

BILL HALEY & HIS COMETS

Bill Haley was born in 1925 in Highland Park, Michigan (love that he was from my neck of the woods). Haley recorded his first song, "Candy Kisses," in 1943. He spent the next four years performing with country and Western bands. In 1949, he became a disc jockey (never trust those guys) at WPWA in Chester, Pennsylvania. There he organized a new band called the Four Aces of Western Swing. Soon after, Haley helped put together another group called Bill Haley and the Saddlemen. After recording a number of lackluster country songs, Haley changed the group's style to a higher-energy rockabilly mode. The group recorded "Rocket 88" and "Rock the Joint" in the early fifties. (One wonders if "Rocket 88" was in reference to Oldsmobile's Rocket 88 car of 1950? I only mention that because, as a small kid, it's the first car I remember that my dad owned. Oh, the memories!)

Haley's program director at WPWA suggested that since they changed their style of music, they needed a name change as well, saying, "Ya know, with a name like Haley, you guys should call your group the Comets," referring to Hailey's Comet. The new name stuck.

In 1953, they recorded an original song from Haley called "Crazy Man, Crazy." That song became the first rock and roll hit to be televised nationally when it was used in a TV show featuring James Dean. In 1954, after taking advice of one of Haley's producers, they covered a song by Sonny Dae from 1952 called "Rock Around the Clock." It wasn't that big of a hit until it became the title track of the movie *Blackboard Jungle*, starring Sidney Portier, in 1955. Many musicologists of popular music history say "Rock Around the Clock" was the first ever rock and roll song of note. Others say it merely brought rock and roll to white America since black audiences already had it down.

Bill and the group then recorded "Shake, Rattle and Roll." While it didn't top "Rock Around the Clock," it was the first rock song to sell a million records.

During their career, the group has been known as Bill Haley & His Comets, Bill Haley's Comets, and Bill Haley & the Comets (take your pick).

My favorite Bill Haley & the Comets songs
'53: "Crazy Man Crazy"
'54: "Rock Around the Clock"
'54: "Shake, Rattle and Roll"
'55: "Dim, Dim the Lights"
'55: "Mambo Rock"
'68: "See You Later, Alligator"

BLUES BROTHERS

A Hollywood movie comedy and millions upon millions of records sold actually started as a skit on the TV show *Saturday Night Live*. John Belushi and Dan Aykroyd put a band together to emulate Sam & Dave and their two big songs, "Soul Man" and "Hold On, I'm Comin'." Belushi and Aykroyd sang lead.

After the movie *Blues Brothers*, the group had hits with several LPs and were featured on several SNL shows.

Belushi died in 1982.

My favorite Blues Bothers songs
"Soul Man"
"Hold On, I'm Comin'"

BOOMTOWN RATS

Original members

Garry Roberts, lead guitar

Johnnie Fingers, keyboards (there's an appropriate name for a keyboard player)

Pete Briquette, bass

Gerry Cott, rhythm guitar

Simon Crowe, drums

I included this group because the name fits. This Irish band became big-time stars in Ireland and the UK, but did not fare well in the US. Much of their unfavorability came as a result of the controversial subject matter in their music.

Their biggest US hit was banned on many radio stations called "I Don't Like Mondays." It was based on a seventeen-year-old girl in San Diego who apparently shot eleven people (two of whom died) on a Monday in 1979. Her excuse was "I don't like Mondays." (Why would someone write a song about some b——h who killed people?)

My favorite Boomtown Rats songs

There are none, zero, zed, nada!

BREAD

Original members

David Gates, vocals, bass, guitar, keyboards, violin, viola, percussion

Jimmy Griffin, vocals, guitar, keyboards, percussion

Robb Royer, vocals, bass, guitar, flute, keyboards, percussion, and recorder

Ron Edgar, drums (that's all?)

Jim Gordon, drums, percussion, piano

Mike Botts, drums (that's all?)

Larry Knechtel (replaced Royer), keyboards, bass, guitar, harmonica

David Gates performed with a group called the Pleasure Fair with Robb Royer and Jimmy Griffin. They signed with Electra Records in January 1969. In 1970, they added a number of other musicians to the group.

They got the name Bread when they noticed a Barbara Ann bread truck in California. For some unknown reason, they decided that would be the appropriate name for their band. (Could have been a different story if the truck was labeled "Let us clean your septic tank"?)

My favorite Bread songs

'70: "Make It with You"

'70: "It Don't Matter to Me"

'72: "Guitar Man"

'77: "Hooked on You"

BRIAN ENO

If you don't recognize this name, I totally understand. But I at least found the eventual name to be somewhat interesting. Brian was born in 1948 in Woodbridge, England, and was a self-described nonmusician. He was a producer and collaborator with a number of groups, including artists such as David Bowie, the Talking Heads, and Devo. Eno used electronics as his instruments. He did play the synthesizer and used his tape recorders to electronically adjust much of the music he produced.

It's easy to figure out why Brian used the name Brian Eno. He was born Brian Peter George Eno. He received his education by the De La Salle Brothers at St. Joseph's College in Ipswich. As a Catholic, when he became confirmed, during a ceremony, he took the name St. John le Baptiste de la Salle, so that his full name now was Brian Peter George St. John de Baptiste de la Salle Eno. (Try putting all that on a business card.) His full name alone made it worthy of including in this endeavor.

BUCKINGHAMS

Original members
- Carl Giammarese, guitar
- Nick Fortuna, guitar
- Curtis Bachman, bass
- Dennis Miccolis, keyboard
- John Poulos, drummer
- George LeGros, vocals
- Dennis Tufano, vocals

This group started in Chicago in 1965 as Giammarese. Fortuna and Bachman joined a band called the Centuries. A few months later, those three left the Centuries and joined another band called the Pulsations, which featured Poulos, LeGros, and Tufano.

In 1966, LeGros (who was drafted—remember, it was the height of the Vietnam War) and Bachman left the group. A little later, WGN-TV in Chicago had a variety show called *All-Time Hits*. The Pulsations became the house band for the show, but producers didn't care for their name. It has been said that a security guard told them they should change the name to the Buckinghams as a tribute to Buckingham Fountain, a Chicago landmark and one of the largest fountains in the world. The band and producers liked it, and the Buckinghams were born.

In 1966, they had their biggest hit, "Kind of a Drag," which hit number 1 and sold over a million copies.

My favorite Buckinghams songs
- '66: "Kind of a Drag"
- '67: "Lawdy Miss Clawdy"
- '67: "Hey Baby (They're Playing Our Song)"
- '67: "Susan"

BUDDY HOLLY AND THE CRICKETS

Charles Hardin Holley (yes, that's the way Holley was spelled initially) was born in Lubbock, Texas, in 1938. Buddy Holly and the Crickets were one of the first groups to popularize the use of two guitars, bass, and drums as a rock and roll band. Buddy also wrote most of his and the Crickets material.

In the early fifties, Holly dropped the *e* from his last name and put together a country band, with his friends in Lubbock, called Buddy Holly and the Two Tunes. The group traveled to Nashville, where they cut several recordings for Decca records, including "Blue Days, Black Nights," "Love Me," "Modern Don Juan," and "Girl on My Mind." None of the songs worked out. They also recorded the country version of "That'll Be the Day." Decca did not release it.

After their failure with Decca, Holly and the Two Tunes returned to Lubbock. At some point, they opened for a young Elvis Presley, who apparently talked Holly into turning his group into a rock and roll band. Holly later said, "We owe it all to Elvis." The group then rerecorded their unreleased song "That'll Be the Day" as a rock tune, and it hit. The group also decided to change their name from Buddy Holly and the Two Tunes. They considered taking a name after birds like so many other groups of that era but decided at first on the name Beeties, but thought better of it and named the group the Crickets. The Beatles were inspired by the group and gave Buddy Holly and the Crickets some credit for their own name (see "Beatles"). In 1957, Buddy Holly and the Crickets became one of the first white groups to perform at the Apollo Theater in New York.

In 1958, Holly split with his group. This resulted in some legal issues for his finances. Those problems prompted Holly to start performing in the Midwest as part of the Winter Dance Party to make some cash. On February 3, 1959, Buddy Holly and two other performers on the tour, Ritchie Valens and J. P. Richardson (The Big Bopper) chartered a plane to take them from Clear Lake, Iowa, to Moorhead, Minnesota. A few minutes after takeoff, the plane crashed, killing all on board, including the pilot, Roger Peterson. It is said that Waylon Jennings was also to be a part of that plane ride but gave his seat to the Big Bopper because Richardson had the flu. That date will live on as "The Day the Music Died" when Don McLean made a song about it in 1971 "American Pie."

Some of my favorite Buddy Holly and the Crickets songs
    '57: "That'll Be the Day"
    '57: "Oh Boy!"
    '57: "Not Fade Away"
    '58: "Maybe Baby"
    '59: "It's So Easy"
    '60: "Peggie Sue"
    '60: "It's Too Late"

BYRDS

Original members
  Jim McGuinn, vocals, lead guitar
  Gene Clark, vocals, tambourine
  David Crosby, vocals, rhythm guitar
  Chris Hillman, vocals, bass
  Michael Clarke, drums

Enormously successful group from the sixties and were said, at one time, to be the US answer to the Beatles. One of their major hits "Turn! Turn! Turn!" was actually taken from a Bible verse.

The Byrds emulated the Beatles with their choice of name because, like the Beatles, who took their name from a bug (like Buddy Holly and the Crickets). They misspelled the name using *Bea* rather than *Bee* in the name. The Byrds did the same switching the *i* for *y*.

My favorite Byrds songs
  '65: "Mr. Tambourine Man"
  '65: "All I Really Want to Do"
  '65: "Turn! Turn! Turn!"

CHICAGO

Original members
    Robert Lamm, vocals, keyboard
    Terry Kath, guitar, vocals
    Walter Parazaider, saxophone
    James Pankow, trombone
    Lee Laughnane, trumpet
    Danny Seraphine, drummer
    Peter Cetera, vocals, bass

Chicago had the distinction in the late sixties of being one of the few rock and roll bands to use brass as an integral part of their group. They originally formed in 1967 under the name the Big Thing. In 1968, James Guercio, who became the group's producer, convinced them to move to Los Angeles. James previously had some success with "Blood Sweat and Tears" and the "Buckinghams."

At that point, Guercio encouraged the Big Thing to change their name to the Chicago Transit Authority from the transportation organization of Chicago. Later, Guercio decided they should shorten their name to just Chicago because there was some speculation that the real Chicago Transit Authority was about to file suit against the group.

Chicago was one of the most successful rock bands of the seventies and beyond. They received ten Grammy nominations, and their first album *Chicago Transit Authority* was inducted into the Grammy Hall of Fame in 2014, and the group itself was inducted into the Rock and Roll Hall of Fame in 2016.

My favorite Chicago songs
    '70: "25 or 6 to 4"
    '70: "Does Anybody Really Know What Time It Is?"
    '71: "Color My World"
    '72: "Saturday in the Park"
    '73: "Feeling Stronger Every Day"

'75: "Old Days"
'76: "Another Rainy Day in New York City"
'76: "If You Leave Me Now"
'77: "You Are on My Mind"

CHI-LITES

Original members
> Eugene Record, lead singer
> Robert "Squirrel" Lester, vocals
> Clarence Johnson, vocals
> Marshall Thompson, vocals
> Creadel "Red" Jones, vocals

The Chi-Lites originally formed out of Chicago in the late fifties from some high school buddies as the Chanteurs and then followed as a trio called Marshall and the Hi-Lites. Soon thereafter, they added a *C* to the equation and became Marshall and the Chi-Lites. The *C* is said to be in tribute to their hometown. Another reason could have been there was another group around already called the Hi-Lites. In 1964, member Clarence Johnson left the group, and they became known as just the Chi-Lites.

The serious interest in this group (both professionally and from a reader's perspective, I hope!) came during a cab ride in Chicago in 1968. The driver of that cab, Eugene Record (hmm, appropriate last name) auditioned for the group and not only became their lead singer but wrote and produced most of their material from that point on. Some (not all) of their hits include "Have you Seen Her?" and "Oh Girl."

The Chi-Lites were inducted into the Rhythm and Blues Foundation in 2000, the Vocal Group Hall of Fame in 2005, and the R & B Music Hall of Fame in 2013. Unfortunately, much of their material was destroyed in the 2008 Universal Hollywood Fire outside of Los Angeles, as was the material of hundreds of other artists.

My favorite Chi-Lites song
> '71: "Have You Seen Her"
> '72: "Oh Girl"

CHUBBY CHECKER

Earnest Evans grew up in Philadelphia in the projects. He worked at a meat and produce market. There are two similar stories regarding how Earnest's name changed.

One story is that Dick Clark had his show called Bandstand in Philadelphia (later to become known as American Bandstand). Somewhere between 1959 and 1960, Clark noticed that the teenagers on the show that danced to the music were doing something new. He asked his producers about it, and was told that Hank Ballard had recorded a song called the "Twist," and that's what it was. Clark considered having Ballard on the show but decided against it because he was known for recording racy songs that had been banned on radio stations across the country. Clark asked his producers to find someone that could do it in his stead. They found and auditioned Earnest Evans. When it was decided they would use him, Clark's wife, Barbara, said, "Earnest Evans won't work as a name, but you remind me of Fats Domino. Let's call you something similar, Chubby Checker" (Dominos, Checkers, smart thinking). The name stuck, and the rest is history.

Another story is that Earnest was given the name Chubby by his boss at the produce market. Chubby used to perform before customers there by doing impressions of popular singers. His boss and his boss's friend (who was a songwriter) brought Chubby to Dick Clark for an audition. He impressed everyone, including Clark's wife, who came up with the idea of adding Checker to his nickname Chubby.

Whether accurate or not, I like the earlier version.

Now, as to the racy songs attributed to Hank Ballard. He had recorded a trilogy of songs in the fifties called his Annie songs. The first was "Work with me, Annie" then "Annie Had a Baby," and finally "Annie's Aunt Fanny." The obvious connotations of those songs were a little too much for the late fifties and were banned by the FCC on radio stations all over the country.

Chubby also had the great fortune to have married Miss World 1962, Catherina Lodders (talk about luck, wow!), for whom he wrote and recorded the song "Loddy Lo."

Interesting note on the "Twist": Chubby's version was number 1 on the Billboard charts in 1960 and again in 1962, the only rock and roll song having done that. Bing Crosby's "White Christmas" did it as well, but obviously it wasn't a rock and roll song.

My favorite Chubby Checker songs
 '60: "The Twist"
 '60: "Whole Lotta Shakin' Goin' On"
 '61: "Pony Time"
 '61: "Let's Twist Again"
 '61: "Jingle Bell Rock"
 '62: "The Twist" (second time it hit number 1)

C. W. McCall

William Dale Fries Jr. loved country music. He worked for an advertising company in 1973 and won a Clio Award for an ad for Old World Bread. The ad featured a trucker named C. W. McCall. The success of that ad inspired Fries to write a song called "Old Home Filler-Up an' Keep on A-Truckin' Café," which Fries sang. At that point, Fries became known as C. W. McCall. In 1976, he sang his biggest hit, "Convoy," which hit number 1 and sold more than two million records. The song was big among CB radio enthusiasts and featured many CB radio phrases.

In 1978, the movie *Convoy* came out and was based on McCall's song.

Fries was also big in environmental and political issues. Fries was actually elected mayor of Ouray, Colorado, in 1986.

Interesting note: McCall released two songs, one called "Kidnap America," referencing the Iranian Hostage crisis, and "Pine Tar Wars," which referred to a 1983 baseball game in which Kansas City Royals player George Brett hit what could have been a game-winning home run. After the homer, Yankees manager Billy Martin (loved this guy when he managed the Detroit Tigers, hated to see him go) came out and complained to the ump that the pine tar on the bat (which many players used) was smeared too far up the bat. The ump agreed and disavowed the hit. That became the last out of the game, and the Yankees were declared winners. (I remember watching the replay of that incident and George was pissed.)

McCall was inducted into the Iowa Rock 'n Roll Hall of Fame in 2009. And "Convoy" is on the list of the top 100 greatest country songs according to *Rolling Stone* magazine.

My favorite C. W. McCall songs
'74: "The Old Home Filler-Up an' Keep on A-Truckin' Café"
'76: "Convoy"

CLARENCE "FROGMAN" HENRY

Clarence was born near New Orleans, Louisiana, in 1937. As a child, he learned to play the piano and later the trombone, where he eventually performed with Bobby Mitchell's New Orleans R & B band. Fats Domino and Professor Longhair are the artists who most influenced him.

It is said that Clarence used his deep croaking voice and his falsetto female voice one night around 1955 in a song called "Ain't Got No Home." A guy named Paul Gayten from Chess Records apparently heard the song and had him record it in 1956. The song hit number 2 on the R & B charts later that year. In the song, Clarence says he "sang like a man, sang like a girl, and sang like a frog." A local DJ named Poppa Stoppa is given credit for dubbing Clarence with the Frogman title after playing the song on the air.

Some of my favorite Clarence "Frogman" Henry songs
'56: "Ain't Got No Home"
'61: "I Don't Know Why I Love You but I Do"
'62: "A Little Too Much"

COASTERS

Original members
  Carl Gardner
  Bobby Nunn
  Billy Guy
  Leon Hughes
  Adolph Jacobs

The Coasters were formed in 1955 from two of the members of the Robins (Carl Gardner and Bobby Nunn). They were called that because they traveled from Los Angeles to the East Coast for a performance. Later, Guy, Hughes, and Jacobs joined the group. Much of their music was written by the famous songwriting team of Leiber and Stoller. Their music was considered on the edge of rhythm and blues and doo-wop.

My favorite Coasters songs
  '55: "Smokey Joe's Café" (as the Robins)
  '57: "Searchin'"
  '57: "Young Bloods"
  '58: "Yakety Yak"
  '58: "Zing! Went the Strings of My Heart"
  '59: "Charlie Brown"
  '59: "Poison Ivy"

COMMANDER CODY AND HIS LOST PLANET AIRMEN

Original members
Commander Cody (Frayne), vocals, keyboard
Billy Farlow, vocals, harmonica
Bill Kirchen, guitar
Andy Stein, sax, fiddle
Paul "Buffalo" Bruce Barlow, bass
Lance Dickerson, drums
Steve "The West Virginia Creeper" Davis, steel guitar
Bobby Black, steel guitar

George Frayne was born in Idaho but began his career in Ann Arbor, Michigan, as a student at U of M. He was not, however, a student of music. His major was in art. Frayne formed his band in 1967, and they began calling themselves Commander Cody and His Lost Planet Airmen. The Commander Cody part of that came from a TV serial whose lead character was Commando Cody. Lost Planet Airmen came from another serial.

My favorite Commander Cody and His Lost Planet Airmen song
'72: "Hot Rod Lincoln"

CONTOURS

Original members
    Joe Billingslea
    Billy Gordon
    Billy Hoggs
    Billy Rollins
    Leroy Fiar (replaced Billy Rollins)
    Hubert Johnson

Joe Billingslea and Billy Gordon started the group in 1959 in Detroit, Michigan. Initially they were called the Blenders. After Leory Fair replaced Billy Rollins, they changed their name to the Contours, a name that was taken from the recording studio they used called Flick and Contour Records.

In 1960, the group auditioned for Motown Records but was turned down by Berry Gordy Jr. Gordy did, however, send them to visit Jackie Wilson, who was related to their bass singer Hubert Johnson. After working with the group, Wilson got them another audition, and this time they were signed to a contract with Motown.

In 1961, the Contours replaced Leroy Fair with Benny Reeves, who was the brother of Martha Reeves. Martha was, believe it or not, doing secretarial work at the time for Hitsville USA (Motown Studios). Benny left the group soon after to join the Navy and was replaced by Sylvester Potts. All during this time, the Contours recorded a number of songs for Motown but did not fare well with any of them until 1962, when they recorded a song Berry Gordy had written called "Do You Love Me." The song sold over a million singles and is the Contours' best claim to fame to this day. In 1988, the song was used in the movie *Dirty Dancing* and became a million-seller all over again. Over time, the Contours had over twenty personnel changes.

My favorite Contours songs
    '62: "Do You Love Me"
    '63: "Shake Sherrie"

CONWAY TWITTY

Harold Lloyd Jenkins was born in 1933 in Mississippi. Jenkins and his family moved to Arkansas when he was ten, and there he formed his first musical group called the Phillips County Ramblers. Jenkins eventually went into radio (never trust those guys). After graduating from high school, Jenkins was offered a chance to play baseball with the Philadelphia Phillies but was drafted into the US Army. While in the service, he formed another group called the Cimmerons.

After his stint in the service, Jenkins began to write music. He worked for a while at Sun Records and heard Elvis Presley's song "Mystery Train," which inspired Jenkins. Around 1957, Jenkins became unhappy with his name and decided he needed a change. One day, he began looking at a road map and found the cities of Conway, Arkansas, and Twitty, Texas. The name stuck, Conway Twitty was born, and the rest is history.

In 1958, Twitty had a hit with "It's Only Make Believe," which was actually the B-side of his record "I'll Try." Twitty continued with success as a rock and roll singer but really wanted to record country music. Unfortunately, many country disc jockeys refused to play his music because he was known as a rock and roll performer.

In 1968, Twitty finally struck a country hit (reaching number 5) with "The Image of Me" and followed that up with his first number 1 country hit called "Next in Line." In 1970, he recorded his biggest country hit, "Hello Darlin'." Twitty followed with many more hits in the next several years.

My favorite Conway Twitty songs
'58: "It's Only Make Believe"
'70: "Hello Darlin'"
'73: "You've Never Been This Far Before"

COUNTRY JOE AND THE FISH

Original members

There are some, but I'm not including them in this because I just don't like them!

This group was regarded as one of the most left-leaning, antiwar bands of the sixties from San Francisco (I think Frisco is probably regarded as the most left-leaning city in the country, so goes to show them being from there). Lead singer Joe McDonald was named after Russian leader Joe Stalin by his parents (go figure, I guess his parents leaned a little to the left too). Joe's first song was "I Seen a Rocket" (apparently Joe missed a few English classes while learning Stalinism). In 1965, Joe met and formed a group with Barry "the Fish" Melton and called themselves Country Mao and the Fish (after Mao Tse-Tung). (There's something that must look good on a résumé!)

The group had the impressive distinction of leading student demonstrations at Berkeley and with their "Fixin to Die Rag" and their "Fish Cheer," which was originally the "F——K Cheer" (I'm sure that made Joe's parents very proud). At this point, they dropped the Mao Tse-Tung reference and became Country Joe and the Fish.

The group was part of the Woodstock Festival in 1969. They were also convicted on an obscenity charge in Massachusetts for leading the infamous "F——K Cheer." In an interesting twist, at least according to one source, the group was paid $10,000 by Ed Sullivan not to appear on his television program. (Hell, sign me up for that one.)

My favorite Country Joe and the Fish songs

Not a one, and I wouldn't put it in here even if I did like one!

COWSILLS

Original members
Bill
Bob
Barry
John
Susan
Paul
Barbara (their mom)

The Cowsills had absolutely nothing to do with cows or sills. The Cowsills started with six brothers (last name Cowsill). Eventually the brothers, sister, and mother also joined the group.

Interesting note: It is said the group was the inspiration for the TV show *The Partridge Family*.

My favorite Cowsills songs
'67: "The Rain, the Park, and Other Things"
'68: "Indian Lake"
'69: "Silver Threads and Golden Needles"

THE CRAZY WORLD OF ARTHUR BROWN

Original members
    Arthur Brown, vocals
    Vincent Crane, keyboards
    Drachen Theaker, drums
    Nick Greenwood, bass

Arthur Brown was in the process of studying law when he began to take an interest in music. He put a band together featuring rock and comedy and called it the Crazy World of Arthur Brown. Brown would often feature himself on stage with his hair burning. He is most famous for a song called "Fire" in 1968.

Hmmm, crazy world, hair burning, and a song called "Fire." See how it all fits so well.

Horrible story here from my days at Honey Radio in the Detroit market. I received a call from one of my regular listeners who had just lost her husband due to a house fire. Needless to say, I felt awful for her. As I was hanging up, I hit the button for the next song. Would you believe it was "Fire" by the Crazy World of Arthur Brown. I felt so bad I looked up her number in our promotional archives and called her to apologize. Terrible!

My favorite Crazy World of Arthur Brown song
    '68: "Fire"

CREAM

Cream was a British rock group formed in 1966 with Eric Clapton, Ginger Baker, and Jack Bruce. The group originally considered naming themselves Sweet 'n' Sour Rock 'n' Roll but changed it to Cream because the trio was considered the cream of the crop in the UK.

My favorite Cream songs
'68: "Sunshine of Your Love"
'68: "White Room"

CREEDENCE CLEARWATER REVIVAL

Original members
  John Fogerty, vocals, guitar
  Tom Fogerty, rhythm guitar
  Stu Cook, bass
  Doug Clifford, drums

CCR began in the late fifties as the Blue Velvets with brothers John and Tom Fogerty and two others all from the same high school. In 1964, they tried for a recording contract as the Golliwogs. That name came from a children's character. In 1968, their new record company manager wanted them to change their name, and the group came up with Creedence Clearwater Revival.

According to members of the group, *Creedence* was the name of a friend of Tom Fogerty, *Clearwater* referred to a beer company's use of "Clear Water," and *Revival* was the band getting back together.

Just an interesting and personal story regarding one of their songs: (at least I hope it's interesting). I was on the air spinning oldies at WOMC radio (Detroit market) in the late nineties. I featured a contest called Ron T's Name That Tune. I would tell listeners if they could name the next tune I was going to play based on a clue I was about to give them, they would win a prize. Well, my clue was, "What do you get when you see Don Phillips [the next DJ coming up] getting up out of his chair while losing his pants at the same time?" Don was there trying to figure it out too! After a commercial break, one of my listeners got it right—"Bad Moon Rising" from CCR (okay, okay, I thought it was cute!).

Some of my favorite CCR songs
  '68: "Suzi Q"
  '68: "I Put a Spell on You"
  '69: "Proud Mary"

'69: "Bad Moon Rising"
'70: "Who'll Stop the Rain"
'70: "Up Around the Bend"

Cuff Links, the Archies, and the Detergents

Original members
  Ron Dante, vocals
  Ron Dante, vocals
  Ron Dante, vocals (read on and you'll understand)

These three groups have something interesting in common: *all* the voices for these groups came from one man—studio singer and radio DJ Ron Dante! Those radio guys are so talented! (Sorry, I had to say that since I spent thirty years in the radio business.)

Apparently Dante would go into a studio and record the lead melodic line vocal of a song then record it again and again and put all the versions together. Then he would go back to the studio and record the harmony voices and put that together with the lead melodies.

You might remember Dante as the Cuff Links with the song "Tracy," "Sugar Sugar" from the Archies, and "Leader of the Laundromat" from the Detergents. Sometime later, Dante stopped recording, and the name Cuff Links was taken up by a group of singers that toured under that name.

My favorite song from these three groups
  '65: "Leader of the Laundromat" (as the Detergents)
  '68: "Sugar Sugar" (as the Archies)
  '69: "Tracy" (as the Cuff Links)

THE DAMNED, THE DEAD BOYS, AND THE DEAD KENNEDYS

All three groups were basically punk rockers, and I don't really care how they got their names (never had any use myself for punk rock) but included them in this section just because of their names.

THE DIAMONDS

Original members
Dave Somerville, lead vocals
Ted Kowalski, tenor
Phil Levitt, baritone
Bill Reed, Bass

The Diamonds were a Canadian group that came out of Toronto, Ontario. Dave Somerville was a sound engineer for the Canadian Broadcasting Corporation and happened to meet the other three members there. After getting together as a quartet, they won first place in the Arthur Godfrey Talent Scout program. That gave them a recording contract with Coral Records. They also appeared on numerous television shows following Arthur Godfrey.

Much of their claim to fame was due to covering black music of the fifties. They recorded "Why Do Fools Fall in Love?" originally from the Teenagers. It was a bigger hit for the Teenagers. Then they recorded "Little Darlin'," originally from the Gladiolas, and "The Stroll" from Chuck Willis. Both covers were more popular for the Diamonds.

There are some stories that suggest one of the members was Amos Hanks, the father of actor Tom Hanks. That turned out *not* to be true. The Diamonds did, however, have several other groups that used their name over the years.

My favorite Diamonds songs
'56: "Why Do Fools Fall in Love?"
'57: "Little Darlin'"
'57: "The Stroll"

DION AND THE BELMONTS

Original members
Dion DiMucci
Angelo D'Aleo
Carlo Mastrangelo
Fred Miano (wow, ya think these guys could be Italian—hey, we stick together)

Dion DiMucci came from the Bronx in New York and started singing at school at the age of five. As a teen, he began getting noticed as a street corner singer. In 1954, Dion made an appearance on the *Teen Club* TV show as a gift to his mother. Following that, he got together with some friends called the Timberlanes, and they recorded a song called "The Chosen Few." Not a big hit!

Later, Dion found some other neighborhood buddies to sing with. The name came from the fact that all lived on or near Belmont Avenue in the Bronx (and probably sang on one those street corners). From that point, they were known as Dion and the Belmonts and became a major sensation. Sometime later, Dion left the group and went on to a successful solo career.

Interesting note: Dion DiMucci was inducted into the Rock and Roll Hall of Fame in 1989. That became a source of contention with the other members, who felt the entire group should have been there. In 2000, they were all inducted into the Vocal Group Hall of Fame, however.

My favorite Dion and the Belmonts songs
'58: "I Wonder Why"
'58: "Teen Angel"
'58: "No One Knows"
'59: "A Teenager in Love"
'59: "When or Where"

DONNA FARGO

Yvonne Vaughan was born and lived much of her life in Mount Airy, North Carolina. She eventually went to college in California, where she settled and married her husband and manager, Stan Silver.

Yvonne became a teacher in California and in her spare time would write and record her own songs. In 1966, Yvonne recorded her first single and adopted the name Donna Fargo. In 1972, her self-written "The Happiest Girl in the Whole USA" was picked up by the DOT label and became a hit in country music as well as Billboard.

Fargo became one of the most successful female country artists of the seventies. She has won a Grammy award, an award from the Country Music Association as well as five awards from the Academy of Country Music.

She still lives with her husband in Nashville, Tennessee, but has had some recent medical issues as of 2019.

My favorite Donna Fargo song
'72: "Happiest Girl in the Whole USA"

DOOBIE BROTHERS

Original members
   Thomas Johnston, vocals, guitar, keyboards
   Patrick Simmons, guitar
   "Little" John Hartman, drums, percussion
   David Shogren, bass
   Michael Hossack, drums
   Jeffrey Allen Baxter, steel guitar

Well, first of all, they weren't brothers at all! Some of the members of the Doobie Brothers started as a group called Pud in the late sixties in San Jose, California. A musician who lived nearby the band suggested they change their name and call themselves the Doobie Brothers, because they were always smoking pot. Interestingly, the members of the group either say they weren't involved in choosing the name or they didn't like the name or didn't know that *doobie* was a term that meant marijuana. (Yeah, right! Maybe their heads were a little fuzzy when the topic came up.) However, the name somehow stuck.

Interestingly the Doobie Brothers played a number of Sunday afternoon jam sessions outside and struck a chord with members of the California Hells Angels motorcycle club, who became huge fans. (That's a good group of fans to have. Keeps you safe.)

The Doobie Brothers have gone through a number of transformations and performed for over five decades. They have over forty million records sold worldwide and were elected to the Vocal Group Hall of Fame in 2004.

My favorite Doobie Brothers songs
   '73: "Long Train Running"
   '73: "China Grove"
   '74: "Another Park, Another Sunday"
   '74: "Black Water"
   '76: "Takin' it to the Streets"

THE DOORS

Original members
    James Douglas Morrison, vocals
    Robert Krieger, guitar
    Raymond Manzarek, bass, keyboards
    John Densmore, drums, keyboards

Jim Morrison put the group together in Los Angeles in 1965. At the time, Morrison was studying film at UCLA when he met Ray Manzarek. Manzarek was a member of a group called Rick and the Ravens and was an accomplished keyboardist. One day on a California beach Morrison read a poem he had written to Manzarek, and he suggested they should work together and put it to music. At that point, they sought the help of other musicians. Guitarist Robby Krieger and drummer John Densmore who were members of the Psychedelic Rangers joined the group.

Morrison suggested they should name their new group the Doors, which was taken from a quote from eighteenth-century poet William Blake in an Aldous Huxley Book, *The Doors of Perception*. The quote reads, "There are things that are known and things that are not known. In between are the Doors."

The group had their problems! After performing, and getting fired, at a local bar called Whiskey a Go Go, it became obvious Morrison had, what some considered to be, serious psychological issues. In 1967, in Connecticut, Jim became the first singer to be arrested on stage during a concert. Morrison was apparently kissing a girl backstage when a cop saw them and told them to leave. Morrison, according to reports, told the cop to "eat it," and he got maced and arrested. (Well, who among us hasn't done that). There was a documentary produced in 2010 about the Doors called *When You're Strange* from their song "People Are Strange."

The Doors released eight albums in just five years. Despite the fact that Morrison was somewhat controversial, many consider their LPs to be some of the greatest of all time. They sold four million albums and nearly eight million singles. All totaled, the Doors sold over thirty-three million records in the US and over one hundred million worldwide. They were inducted into the Rock and Roll Hall of Fame in 1993. Morrison died in 1971. To this day, it is unclear exactly what happened.

My favorite Doors songs
    '67: "Light My Fire"
    '67: "People are Strange"
    '68: "Hello, I Love You"
    '68: "Touch Me"
    '71: "Love Her Madly"
    '71: "Riders on the Storm"

DRIFTERS

Original members
> Clyde McPhatter, lead vocals
> Gerhart Thrasher, tenor
> Andrew Thrasher, baritone
> Bill Pickney, bass
> Jimmy Oliver, guitar

Note: McPhatter was replaced by David Baughan in 1954, who was replaced by Johnny Moore in 1955, who was replaced by Bobby Hendricks in 1957.

Ben E. King came along as lead in 1958 replaced by Rudy Lewis in 1961, who was replaced by the return of Johnny Moore in 1964. (There were many more replacements over the years, but that might require another book.)

This group was originally a backup group for Clyde McPhatter. According to most reports, the Drifters got their name because members of the group *drifted* from a variety of bands before getting together. They established themselves in 1953 with lead singer Clyde McPhatter, who was previously with the Dominoes. They had a number of hits in a short amount of time. One year later, McPhatter was drafted into the army.

After a number of personnel changes, the manager of the group, George Treadwell (who had rights to the Drifters name), put another Drifters group together featuring Ben E. King. That group was originally known as the Five Crowns. After a number of hits, King left the group for a solo career, and Rudy Lewis was brought in to replace him. Again, the group had a number of hits until Lewis died in 1964. Johnny Moore, one of the original members, then rejoined the group as lead singer sang one of their biggest hits, "Under the Boardwalk."

From that point on, a number of groups calling themselves the Drifters performed in the US and overseas. Some still perform to this day. It is said that as many as sixty singers were part of the Drifters at one time or another.

My favorite Drifters songs
'58: "There Goes My Baby"
'60: "This Magic Moment"
'60: "Save the Last Dance for Me"
'61: "Some Kind of Wonderful"
'62: "Up on the Roof"
'63: "On Broadway"
'64: "Saturday Night at the Movies"
'64: "Under the Boardwalk"

DUSTY SPRINGFIELD

In her early life, Mary Isobel Catherine O'Brien grew up in Buckinghamshire, England, and later attended St. Anne's Convent School. Apparently, Mary and her brother became frustrated with their parents and became known as food throwers, even as adults. (Well, who among us hasn't thrown a brussels sprout or two across the table once in a while?) At one point in her life, Mary enjoyed playing football (probably soccer rather than American football) with the boys, and she was known as a tomboy. Because of that, she was given the nickname Dusty.

At one point, Mary put together a female group, calling themselves the Lana Sisters. In 1959, Mary left the sisters and began singing as a trio with her brother, Dionysius O'Brien, and another guy, Tim Field. Dion called himself Tom Springfield, so the three called themselves the Springfields. The Springfields had some hits but broke up in 1963.

Later in 1963, Mary decided to go solo and began to use her nickname Dusty and also took the name of the trio that was disbanded, Springfield. Dusty Springfield was born. Dusty became the UK's biggest female music star in the midsixties. Interesting note: In the mid- to late sixties, Dusty would fill in as a backup singer for a number of groups, but she used the name (get this) Glady's Thong! (Hmmmm, wish I had a picture!)

My favorite Dusty Springfield songs
'64: "I Only Want to Be with You"
'64: "Wishin' and Hopin'"
'66: "You Don't Have to Say You Love Me"
'66: "All I See Is You"
'67: "The Look of Love"
'69: "Don't Forget About Me"
'69: "The Windmills of Your Mind"

EARTH, WIND & FIRE

Original members
> Maurice White, vocals, percussion
> Verdine White, bass, percussion
> Philip Bailey, vocals, percussion
> Ralph Johnson, drums
> Larry Dunn, keyboards
> Al McKay, guitar, sitar, percussion
> John Graham, guitar, percussion
> Andrew Woolfolk, sax, flute
> Jessica Cleaves, drums, percussion

Earth, Wind & Fire was started by Maurice White in 1969 out of Chicago. White began as a gospel singer in high school. He joined up with friends Wade Flemons and Don Whitehead. They originally called themselves the Salty Peppers.

After a number of deletions and additions to the group and a move to Los Angeles, they decided to change their name. The new name came from White's astrological sign, Sagittarius. Apparently, the sign has primary elements of fire and earth and air, depending on where you are located on the globe and what season it is. The group was also helped along the way by National Football League great Jim Brown, who was a former running back for the Cleveland Browns (many call him the greatest running back of all time—I'm sticking with Barry Sanders, though) and was now working to find worthwhile talent for investors.

Earth, Wind & Fire have an incredible number of awards and accolades. They include six Grammys, four American Music Awards, a Grammy Lifetime Achievement Award, and a Congressional Horizon Award. They are members of the Rock and Roll Hall of Fame and the Vocal Group Hall of Fame and have a star on the Hollywood Walk of Fame. Earth, Wind & Fire has sold over ninety million records. Maurice White died in 2014.

My favorite Earth, Wind & Fire songs
'75: "Sing a Song"
'76: "Can't Hide Love"
'76: "Saturday Nite"

ELECTRIC LIGHT ORCHESTRA

Original members
  Jeff Lynne, vocals, Moog synthesizer, guitar
  Richard Tandy, guitar, keyboards
  Michael Edwards, cello
  Colin Walker, cello
  Will Gibson, violin
  Michael Albuquerque, bass
  Bev Bevan, drums
  Roy Wood, many instruments

The Electric Light Orchestra, or ELO as it would be called began in 1970 in Birmingham, England. Musicians Jeff Lynne, Roy Wood, and Bev Bevan started as a group called the Move. Later they changed the name to ELO. Their idea was to incorporate classical instruments into their music, like violins, cellos, basses, woodwinds, and brass.

The name of the group was not all that significant, but the name of their first LP in the US was sort of interesting. The name was "The Electric Light Orchestra" (real original, right?). It was released in the UK and elsewhere under that name. However, in the US, the record company secretary thought it was just the name of the album and tried to call them to get the name of the group as well. She couldn't get anyone to answer the phone, so she left a note, "No Answer." You got it! The first ELO album in the US was called *No Answer*. I hope that secretary got a bonus or some residual payment for naming the LP.

My favorite ELO songs
  '73: "Roll Over Beethoven"
  '74: "Can't Get It Out of My Head"
  '75: "Evil Woman"
  '78: "Sweet Talkin' Woman"

ELECTRIC PRUNES

Original members
James Lowe, vocals, guitar
Mark Tulin, bass
Ken Williams, guitar
Michael "Quint" Weakley, drums
Dick Hargrave, keyboard

The Electric Prunes were largely a psychedelic rock band featuring fuzz-tones and sound effects. They started in 1965 as a garage band called the Sanctions and then later as Jim and the Lords.

Record producer David Hassinger suggested the group should change their name. One of the members suggested the name the Electric Prunes (that seemed like a logical name for a psycho band). The group first thought the name was a joke, and vocalist James Lowe said they considered a number of alternatives. In the end, Lowe said, "It's the one thing everyone will remember, it's not attractive, and there's nothing sexy about it, but people won't forget it." From that point on, the name stuck.

In 1967, the group disbanded, and a new group with the name Electric Prunes began to record religious songs.

Songs to remember
'66: "I Had Too Much to Dream (Last Night)"
'66: "Get Me to the World on Time"

New Group in '67 with mostly new members recording religious songs
'68: "Mass in F Minor"

ELTON JOHN

Reginald Kenneth Dwight was born in 1947 in Middlesex, England. Dwight learned to play the piano as a child and at the age of fifteen joined a band called John Baldry's Bluesology to become their organ player. That group would be instrumental in changing Dwight's name.

Before the group parted ways in 1967, Dwight figured he needed a better stage name, so he took the first names of two of the members of the band, Elton from Elton Dean, the group's saxophonist, and John from John Baldry's Bluesology. He took the first names of both, and there you go, Elton John was born!

There are so many superlatives regarding John's career they are far too numerous to mention, but here's just a few. John has sold over three hundred million records and has been given nearly every musical award there is. John has received Grammy Awards, Brit Awards, an Academy Award, a Golden Globe, a Tony, and a Disney Legends Award and was honored at the Kennedy Center to name some of his biggest!

He was also knighted by Queen Elizabeth II for "services to music and charitable services." *Sir Elton Hercules John* is so highly regarded he was selected to perform at the funeral of Princess Diana in 1997 at Westminster Abbey and for the Queen's Diamond Jubilee Concert at Buckingham Palace in 2012.

Sir John was also instrumental in the fight against AIDs, as has raised close to five hundred million dollars in that effort! The word *superstar* most definitely fits, but even that is hardly enough.

Favorite Elton John songs
Let's face it, just about every one of them!

EMOTIONS

Original members
    Sheila Hutchinson
    Wanda Hutchinson
    Jeanette Hutchinson

This was a sister act that began with Wanda, Sheila, and Jeanette Hutchinson along with their father, Joe. They performed gospel music in a number of churches, with Dad, for a number of years, as the Heavenly Sun Beams. They also performed as Three Ribbons and a Bow (Dad was the beau). The girls even sang on the *Jerry Van Dyke Children's Gospel* TV show.

While touring, they met the Staples, and it was apparently that group that convinced them to change their name to the Emotions. The Staples helped them get a recording contract, and at that time, they began concentrating on secular music rather than gospel. They became one of the most influential R & B girl groups of all time.

Best singles
    '76: "Flowers"
    '76: "I Don't Wanna Lose Your Love"
    '77: "Best of My Love"

ENCHANTMENT

Original members
    David Banks
    Emanuel "EJ" Johnson
    Edgar "Micky" Clanton
    Bobbi Green
    Joe "Jobie" Thomas

This group started in 1966 at Detroit's Pershing High School with David Banks, Emanuel Johnson, Edgar Clanton, Bobbi Green, and Joe Thomas. I have no clue how they came up with the name Enchantment, but since they were from the east side of Detroit (where I grew up), I decided to include them. The group had hits starting in 1977.

Songs of note
    '77: "Gloria"
    '77: "Sunshine"
    '78: "It's You That I Need"

ENGELBERT HUMPERDINCK

Arnold George Dorsey was born in India in 1936. At the age of ten, he and his parents moved to Leicester, England, where he began to take up an interest in music. That's where he decided to try playing the saxophone and did so at various events and nightclubs. In his late teens, Dorsey was pushed to try his hand (and voice) at singing and did an impression of Jerry Lewis. His friends then started calling him Gerry Dorsey, and the name stuck till Dorsey was in his late twenties. After a couple years in the British Army, Dorsey came back to singing at local clubs and venues.

In the midsixties, Dorsey met up with a guy named Gordon Mills, who managed the likes of Tom Jones and others. It was Mills who suggested a name change and came up with Engelbert Humperdinck (that's not the first name that would come to my mind, but what the hell, it worked, and what do I know?). The name was actually taken from a nineteenth-century German opera composer. And the rest, as they say, is history.

Unfortunately, Engelbert was struck with tuberculosis in 1961, but he recovered nicely. His biggest break came in 1967 with the release of "Release Me," which hit the top 10 in both the US and England. Engelbert was particularly sought after by his female fans, who called themselves Humperdinckers (my mind is going all over the place with that one).

Some of my favorite Engelbert Humperdinck songs
'67: "Release Me"
'67: "There Goes My Everything"
'67: "The Last Waltz"
'68: "A Man without Love"

FANNY

Original members
    June Millington, guitar, vocals
    Jean Millington, bass, vocals
    Addie Lee, guitar, vocals
    Brie Brandt, drums, vocals
    Alice de Buhr, drums, vocals (replaced Brandt)
    Nickey Barclay, keyboard, vocals

This group was started by two girls in high school in California. June and Jean Millington were born in Manila in the Philippines and were daughters of a Navy sailor, who was then transferred to Sacramento. The girls asked two other girls, Addie Lee and Brie Brandt, to join with them and form a group. The Svelts was born. Then in 1968, they bought a bus and decided to tour the coast as Wild Honey.

After a few personnel changes, including Nickey Barclay on keyboard, Wild Honey decided they would perform one more gig before giving up on their musical careers. It just happened to be open mic night at the Troubadour Club in Los Angeles. Music producer Richard Perry's secretary was at the club and suggested he take a look at them. Perry liked what he heard and got them a recording contract with Reprise Records.

It is said that George Harrison suggested that Wild Honey change their name to Fanny, although without the sexual connotation (of course!). Fanny was one of the first notable, all-female rock groups of the 1970s.

My favorite Fanny songs
    '70: "Badge"
    '72: "Hey Bulldog"
    '72: "Ain't That Peculiar"

FATS DOMINO

Fats was born in New Orleans, Louisiana, in 1928 as Antoine Domino Jr. At the age of ten, Fats learned to play the piano with the help of his brother-in-law, Harrison Verrett. As a young teenager, Domino was performing in local bars. A few years later, he came to the attention of bandleader Billy Diamond. Diamond liked what he heard and invited Domino to join his band, the Solid Senders.

Diamond is responsible for coming up with the name Fats Domino because he reminded him of two other rotund pianists, Fats Pichon and Fats Waller, and of course, Domino was a little round as well.

Fats and his wife, Rosemary, were together from 1947 till her death in 2008, and they had eight kids. You might get the impression Fats likes *A* names cause his kids were named Antoine III, Anatola, Andre, Antonio, Antoinette, Andrea, Anola, and Adonica. Fats died in 2017.

In my early twenties, I saw Fats perform at the Sahara Hotel in Las Vegas in a small room at about 2:00 a.m. with only a dozen or so people there. He performed anything anyone wanted to hear. Obviously, a great show!

Some of Fats's hundreds of songs (these are my favorites)
>'55: "Ain't That a Shame"
>'56: "Blueberry Hill"
>'56: "Blue Monday"
>'57: "I'm Walkin'"
>'59: "I Want to Walk You Home"
>'60: "Walking to New Orleans"

THE FEELIES

Original members
    Glenn Mercer, vocals, guitar
    Bill Million, percussion
    Dave Weckerman, percussion
    Richard Reilly, vocals
    Vinny DeNunzio, percussion
    John Papesca, bass
    Anton Fier, drums

This group was not very successful, at least commercially, but is said to have substantially influenced the American rock genre. The Feelies (every time a see that name, I look at my own hands, don't know exactly why) formed in 1976 and released four LPs in their early years.

The name Feelies actually came from the book *Brave New World* by Aldous Huxley. It was a futuristic entertainment device taken from that book.

My favorite Feelies songs
    Sorry, I don't really have any.

FLEETWOOD MAC

Original members
Peter Green, lead guitar
John McVie, bass
Jeremy Spencer, guitar
Mick Fleetwood, drums, percussion
Daniel Kinwan, guitar
Stevie Nicks, vocals

This group got together in London, England, in 1967. Peter Green and Mick Fleetwood worked together in three other groups. One was Peter B's Looners, another was Shotgun Express, and the third was John Mayall & the Bluesbreakers.

It was Green who suggested to Fleetwood that they put a new band together. They both wanted the Bluesbreakers bass player John McVie to join them. They tried to entice him by suggesting the name of the group would be Fleetwood Mac. The *Mac* portion would be based on his name McVie. However, McVie decided he didn't want to take the risk, so they hired another bass player, Bob Brunning, to the band with the understanding that if McVie ever decided to join them, he would have to leave. Brunning agreed! Within just a few weeks, McVie did decide he wanted to be part of the group and Brunning left. Fleetwood Mac was born.

Fleetwood Mac is one of the world's best-selling bands, having sold more than 120 million records. They received a star on the Hollywood Walk of Fame and were inducted into the Rock and Roll Hall of Fame in 1998. Members of the group also performed for the Bill Clinton Presidential Inauguration in 1993.

My favorite Fleetwood Mac songs
'75: "Over My Head"
'76: "Say Your Love Me"
'76: "Go Your Own Way"
'77: "You Make Lovin' Fun"

THE FLEETWOODS

Original members
    Gary Troxel
    Gretchen Christopher
    Barbara Ellis

This trio (two women, one man) from Olympia, Washington, had two number 1 songs in 1959, "Come Softly to Me" and "Mr. Blue." Since Fleetwood is a model of Cadillac. It has been suggested, like the Cadillacs, the Edsels, the Eldorados, and the Hondells that they got their name from the car. But no! Actually, the Fleetwoods got their name from the phone number of one of their members. Those of us with a few years under our belts will remember that, back in the day, our phone numbers had a word in front of it. I still remember my number in Detroit in the late fifties was Venice-92081 and would be dialed as VE-9-2081. Their number would be Fleetwood and dialed as FL-*-****. Just to have a hint of accuracy, though, Fleetwoods are awfully nice automobiles, especially in 1959.

The Fleetwoods were inducted into the Vocal Group Hall of Fame and the Doo Wop Hall of Fame in 2006. They were also inducted into the Northwest Area Music Association Hall of Fame in 1988.

My favorite Fleetwoods songs
    '59: "Come Softly to Me"
    '59: "Mr. Blue"

FOREIGNER

Original members
    Mick Jones
    Ian McDonald
    Lou Gramm
    Dennis Elliot
    Al Greenwood
    Ed Gagliardi

This group came up with the name Foreigner because three of the members, Lou Gramm, Ed Gagliardi, and Al Greenwood, were from New York City here in the US and three were from London, England, Mick Jones, Ian McDonald, and Dennis Elliot.

My favorite Foreigner songs
    '77: "Feels Like the First Time"
    '77: "Cold as Ice"

FOUR SEASONS

Original members
>   Frankie Valli, vocals
>   John Paiva, guitar
>   Don Ciccone, bass
>   Bob Gaudio, keyboards
>   Lee Shapiro, keyboards
>   Gerry Polci, vocals, drums

Frances Casteluccio, better known as Frankie Valli, and at one time Frankie *Valley*, started his career in the early fifties. Valli and his friends performed in the Newark, New Jersey, area under the vocal names the Romans, the Varitones, and others. Later they settled on the name the Four Lovers. In 1960, the Lovers auditioned at a bowling alley in New Jersey and did *not* get picked. Newly acquired keyboardist and singer Bob Gaudio suggested they get something out of the experience and take the name of the bowling alley, Four Seasons, and it stuck. Bob Gaudio was formerly from the Royal Teens and wrote their hit song "Short Shorts."

The Four Seasons were incredibly successful and did so despite the effects of the British Invasion, which depressed so many American groups during that time. They also recorded under a few different names, the most notable the Wonder Who, and recorded "Don't Think Twice" under that name.

The Four Seasons were inducted into the Rock and Roll Hall of Fame in 1990 and the Vocal Group Hall of Fame in 1999. The group has sold an estimated one hundred million records around the world. As of 2018, Frankie Valli still performs with the Four Seasons (though with none of the original members).

(As a personal footnote, I had the opportunity to emcee two of their concerts in the Detroit area some years ago. Might as well blow my own horn a bit.)

Some of the Four Seasons greatest hits
    '62: "Sherry"
    '62 "Walk Like a Man"
    '62: "Candy Girl"
    '63: "Big Girls Don't Cry"
    '64: "Dawn"
    '64: "Rag Doll"
    '65: "Don't Think Twice" (as the Wonder Who)
    '76: "December of 1963 (Oh What a Night)"
    And many, many others

FOUR TOPS

Original members
Levi Stubbs, lead vocals
Abdul "Duke" Fakir, backup vocals
Renaldo "Obie" Benson, backup vocals
Lawrence Payton, backup vocals

The members of this outstanding Motown group were all from the Motor City and met in high school in the early fifties. During that time, they attended a party and, for fun, started to harmonize with an R & B sound. The reaction was so strong and positive they figured they would join forces and start a group. They became known as the Four Aims. In 1956, Chess Records signed the group, but to limited success. They also recorded for Red Top Records, Riverside, and Columbia, also with limited success.

In 1963, the Four Aims ran into Berry Gordy Jr. (a friend of theirs), and he asked them to join his new label, Motown Records. A year later, they decided to switch from R & B to pop and began working with Holland, Dozier, Holland (also with the Motown label). At this point, the group changed their name to the Four Tops. Their first release as a pop group was "Baby I Need Your Loving," and that was the first of dozens of hits on the label. It is said, quite accurately, that the Four Tops helped define the Motown label.

Humiliating note: I once interviewed Four Top original member, Duke Fakir, and mistakenly mispronounced his name as Duke Faker. Ouch! At least he got a laugh out of it.

My favorite Four Tops songs
'64: "Baby I Need Your Loving"
'65: "Ask the Lonely"
'66: "Shake Me, Wake Me"
'66: "Reach Out, I'll Be There"
'66: "Standin in the Shadows of Love"
'67: "Bernadette"

FREDDIE "BOOM BOOM" CANNON

Freddie Picariello grew up on the east coast listening to R & B music and based his own style in that way. He was inspired by the likes of Big Joe Turner, Chuck Berry, Little Richard, and Bo Diddley. In the late fifties, Freddie appeared on *Boston Ballroom*, a local TV show as Freddie and the Hurricanes.

His biggest hit actually began as a song called "Rock N Roll Baby," written by Freddie's mom! It was then rewritten and renamed as "Tallahassee Lassie." After some rejections, Dick Clark, from *American Bandstand*, listened to it and with some edits had Freddie present it on his show. At that point, he took the name Freddie Cannon for his booming style of singing and soon after became known as Freddie "Boom Boom" Cannon.

Dick Clark liked Freddie so much he became a regular on *American Bandstand* and made over a hundred appearances on the show.

An interesting note: After finishing a show in London, Freddie and his father were offered a ride to the airport from Eddie Cochran, who also performed there. They weren't ready and turned the ride down. A little later, they heard Eddie died in a car crash on the way.

My favorite Freddi Cannon songs
    '62: "Palisades Park"
    '62: "Where the Action Is" (theme song from the TV show)

FREDDIE FENDER

Freddie's real name was actually Baldemar Garza Huerta. He was born in 1937 and passed away in 2006 from lung cancer. He is best known as a solo singer/guitarist and performed with the groups Los Super Seven and the Texas Tornados.

Freddie, or Baldemar, actually spent three years as a US Marine starting when he was seventeen. He became well-known in Texas for his rockabilly-style music. In 1958, he decided he needed a name change so he would "sell better with Gringos!" so he made the change to Freddie Fender. Fender was selected because he played a Fender guitar, and Freddie because he liked the alliteration.

My favorite Freddie Fenders songs
'75: "Before the Next Teardrop Falls"
'75: "Wasted Days and Wasted Nights"

Gary Puckett & the Union Gap

Original members
Gary "General" Puckett, lead vocals, guitar
Dwight "Sergeant" Bement, sax
Gary "Private" Withem, keyboards
Kerry "Corporal" Chater, bass
Paul "Private" Wheatbread, drums

This group was organized by Gary Puckett during the midsixties. After dropping out of Diego State College, Puckett played in a variety of bands, including the Outcasts and Gary & the Remarkables. In 1967, they renamed themselves the Union Gap and recostumed themselves in Union Army Civil War uniforms. Gary would be decked out in a general's uniform while other members were a sergeant, corporal, and privates. The name Union Gap came from the name of a small town of the same name in Washington State.

In 1966, Paul Wheatbread (hmm, makes me hungry) became the drummer on the television series *Where the Actions Is*. (I only mention that because I used to love that show.) Later, Wheatbread rejoined Gary and the rest of the group again.

Gary Puckett & the Union Gap had several big hits throughout the late sixties. Their first single "Woman, Woman" became their first hit and sold over a million records. That was followed by "Young Girl," "Lady Willpower," and "Over You," which all became top 10 hits.

My favorite Gary Puckett & the Union Gaps songs
'67: "Woman, Woman"
'68: "Young Girl"
'68: "Lady Willpower"
'69: "This Girl Is a Woman Now"

GARY U.S. BONDS

Gary Anderson started as a street corner doo-wop singer in the midfifties out of Jacksonville, Florida. He sang then with a group called the Turks. He got together with his manager, Frank Guida, and they released a number of singles. Their first national hit came in late 1960 called "New Orleans." Guida had given him the name U.S. Bonds without him even knowing it. They were apparently trying to take advantage of people thinking it had something to do with government bonds. (Go figure.) Later they added Gary to the mix for Gary U.S. Bonds.

My favorite Gary U.S. Bonds songs
    '60: "New Orleans"
    '61: "Quarter to Three"

GLADYS KNIGHT AND THE PIPS

Original members
  Gladys Knight
  Merald "Bubba" Knight, brother
  Brenda Knight, sister
  Eleanor Guest, cousin
  William Guest, cousin

This group was pretty much all family members from Atlanta, Georgia. Gladys Knight actually began her career in the early fifties at four years old. She sang with a number of choirs at a variety of churches while touring in the Atlanta area. In 1952, at the age of seven, she won first prize on the Ted Mack's *Amateur Hour*. Another important event took place in 1952. Gladys' brother, Bubba, was celebrating his tenth birthday, and at that party, the record player they wanted to use did not work. To make up for the misfortune, Gladys, Bubba, and their sister, Brenda, along with cousins Eleanor and William started singing. A great group was born.

Soon after their birthday performance and under the direction of Gladys's mother, Elizabeth, they agreed to form a quintet. After considering other names, they settled on the Pips, which was a nickname of another cousin, James "Pip" Woods. Woods encouraged the group to go professional. By 1957, the Pips was the opening act for recording greats like Jackie Wilson and Sam Cooke.

In 1961, the group was dealing with two different record labels and had a hit with "Every Beat of My Heart" on both. At this point, the Pips changed their name to Gladys Knight and the Pips. But things started to change again. Gladys left the group for a while because she got married and then had two children. She married Jimmy Newman and gave birth to their son, James, and later in 1963 to their daughter, Kenya. Gladys did begin performing again but as a solo artist and then later reunited with the Pips.

Gladys Knight and the Pips enjoyed huge success through the sixties and seventies. They were inducted into the Rock and Roll Hall of Fame in 1996 and the Vocal Group Hall of Fame in 2001. They had several other distinctions, such as membership in the Rhythm and Blues Hall of Fame and the Apollo Theater's Hall of Fame.

Gladys also had other eggs to fry and made her acting debut in 1977 in a movie called *Pipe Dreams*. That was a love story set in the Alaskan pipeline area. Later, because of some legal issues, Gladys was not allowed to record with the Pips for several years but did sing live with them.

My favorite Gladys Knight and the Pips songs
    '61: "Every Beat of My Heart"
    '67: "Heard It through the Grapevine"
    '67: "Friendship Train"
    '67: "If I Were Your Woman"
    '73: "Neither One of Us"
    '73: "Midnight Train to Georgia"
    '74: "The Way We Were"

GRAND FUNK RAILROAD

Original members
    Mark Farner, vocals, guitar
    Don Brewer, vocals, drums
    Mel Schacher, bass
    Craig Frost, keyboards

Grand Funk Railroad (shortened to Grand Funk) was one of the most popular concert groups of the late sixties and seventies. They started as the Jazz Masters out of Flint, Michigan. They also became known as the Pack after Terry Knight of Terry Knight and the Pack, who became their manager. It was Knight who decided they needed a different name. He called them Grand Funk Railroad, a play on words on a Michigan-based rail line, Grand Trunk Western Railroad.

Unfortunately, Grand Funk Railroad was one of dozens of bands who lost their material in the infamous fire at Universal Studios in Hollywood in 2008.

My favorite Grand Funk songs
    '70: "Heartbreaker"
    '73: "We're an American Band"

GRATEFUL DEAD

Original members
 Jerry Garcia, vocals, guitar
 Bob Weir, vocals, rhythm guitar
 Ron "Pigpen" McKernan, vocals, keyboards, harmonica
 Phil Lesh, vocals, bass
 Bill Kreutzmann, drums

The Grateful Dead formed in Palo Alto, California, in 1965. They were one of the most popular rock bands to come out of the San Francisco Bay Area. Members of the group performed under the names the Zodiacs, the Wildwood Boys, and Mother McCree's Uptown Jug Champions (I'd love to know how they got that name). Later they would be known as the Warlocks.

In 1966, the group decided to change their name to the Grateful Dead while apparently under the influence of acid. The drug was legal in California at that time. According to the group's bass player, Phil Lesh, it was Jerry Garcia who found the name in a dictionary and suggested, "Hey, man, how about the Grateful Dead?" However, it happened, and the name stuck. Hard-core fans of the group are known as Dead Heads. (I wonder if they might have been hittin' the acid too!)

Early albums
 The Grateful Dead
 Anthem of the Sun
 Live/Dead

GUESS WHO

Original members
   Chad Allan, guitar, vocals (real name Allan Kowbel—wow, that name will ring your chimes)
   Bob Ashley, keyboards
   Randy Bachman, guitar, vocals
   Jim Kale, bass, vocals
   Garry Peterson, drums, vocals

This group originated from Winnipeg, Manitoba, Canada, in 1958 as Allen and the Silvertones. Later the name changed to Chad Allen and the Reflections. In 1965, the name changed again because an American group called the Reflections (who happen to be good friends of mine) had a hit song with "Just Like Romeo and Juliet." The group then became known as Chad Allen and the Expressions. In 1965, the group released their single "Shakin' All Over," which reached number 1 in Canada and number 22 in the States.

This is where it gets interesting! Their American label, Sceptor, released "Shakin' All Over" and tried to work up interest by not naming the group, but suggesting DJs ask their audiences, "Guess who does this great song?" After the label released the real name as Chad Allen and the Expressions, disc jockeys ignored it and continued to use the name the Guess Who. And that's the name that stuck.

Interestingly again, sometime later, the Four Seasons tried the same thing and released some of their music as from the Wonder Who. (Hmmm, *I wonder who* did this? Anything to get mentioned on the air.)

The Guess Who became Winnipeg's leading rock band and even had their own TV show called *Where It's At*.

The Guess Who was inducted into the Canadian Music Hall of Fame in 1987, and many members of the group received the Governor General's Performing Arts Award for Lifetime Achievement in 2002.

My favorite Guess Who songs
'65: "Shakin' All Over"
'69: "No Time"
'69: "These Eyes"
'69: "Laughing"
'70: "American Woman"

HANK BALLARD

Hank Ballard was born in Detroit. The only reason I write about him is his rather racy story. Hank Ballard and the Midnighters actually originated the "Twist" a year before Chubby Checker. When Dick Clark noticed the kids on his TV show *American Bandstand* were doing this "different" dance, he asked his producers about it. They told him they were doing the twist, a song by Hank Ballard and the Midnighters. Clark said he couldn't have Ballard on the show because of all his racy songs (banned on radio stations in much of the US). He needed someone singing the "Twist" that wasn't Ballard to appear on the show. (Please see Chubby Checker.)

Here's the risqué part of the story. In the midfifties, Ballard recorded his trilogy of Annie songs: "Work with Me, Annie" (a little imagination is all it takes to figure that one out), "Annie Had a Baby" (the result of the first one), and Annie's Aunt Fanny (Aunt Fanny's reaction to issues of the first two). They were his biggest hits and sold over a million copies across the world even though they were banned from radio here in the US. In 1974, Ballard recorded "Let's Go Streaking."

He recorded the song in the *nude*! (And I don't mean in the shower.) Now, try to get that image out of your mind.

Despite the interesting twist to the Ballard story, he was inducted into the Rock and Roll Hall of Fame in 1990. The Midnighters were inducted into the hall of fame in 2012. Interesting note: Ballard's cousin Florence Ballard became a member of Motown legends the Supremes.

Ballard died in 2003 of throat cancer.

My favorite Hank songs
'54: "Work with Me, Annie"
'54: "Annie Had a Baby"
'54: "Annie's Aunt Fanny"
'59: "The Twist"
'74: "Let's Go Streaking (Did I Ever? I'll Never Tell)"

THE HAPPENINGS

Original members
> Bob Miranda
> David Libert
> Tom Guiliano
> Ralph Divito
> Bernie LaParta (replaced Divito in 1968)
> Lenny Conforti, drums

This group began in the early sixties as the Four Graduates. Although one source says they began in the military at Fort Dix, New Jersey; lead vocalist Bob Miranda says they started in the men's room in central high school in Paterson, New Jersey. Following that flushing endeavor, they played at a number of small local venues just to get exposure. Then at one point, they ran into members and producers of the Tokens and joined the group's record label, B. T. Puppy.

At this point, the group decided they needed a name change and considered a number of options. They thought about the Corduroys (yeah, they were big in the sixties, the pants, not the group) and the Bitter Lemons, but no one liked them (must have left a funny taste in their mouths) and decided on the Happenings. Their first release, with the new name, was in 1965 called "Girls on the Go," which was a moderate hit (and that's being nice) in the northeast, and that was about it. Then came 1966, and "See You in September" became a huge hit with longevity! The song was not an original and was actually a moderate hit for the Tempos back in 1959.

Some of my favorite hits from the Happenings
> '66: "See You in September"
> '66: "Go Away Little Girl"
> '67: "Why Do Fools Fall in Love?"
> '68: "Breaking Up Is Hard to Do"

HARPERS BIZARRE

Original members
Ted Templeman, vocals, drums, guitar
Dick Scoippettone, vocals, guitar, bass
Eddie James, guitar
Dick Yount, vocals, bass
John Petersen, vocals, percussion

This group was formed in 1963 from Santa Cruz, California, as the Tikis and became known locally in the San Francisco market as the beginning of the Love Generation. Their popularity soared with their one major pop hit "The 59th Street Bridge Song (Feelin' Groovy)," an original from Simon and Garfunkel.

The song was then rereleased as the group changed their name to Harpers Bizarre. The name was based on the magazine called *Harper's Bazaar* (note the change in spelling). The song hit 13 on the Billboard Hot 100 chart and was the group's biggest hit. Later their song "Chattanooga Choo Choo" reached number 1 on the Easy Listening chart.

Interesting note: After performing in Pasadena, California, in 1969, their flight back to San Francisco was hijacked. Passengers were released, but the plane and crew flew on to Rome, Italy, where the hijacker was caught. It is said to be the farthest distance for an airplane hijacking.

Favorite Harpers Bizarre songs
'67: "The 59th Street Bridge Song (Feelin' Groovy)"
'67: "Chattanooga Choo Choo"

HERMAN'S HERMITS

Original members
> Keith Hopwood, vocals, rhythm guitar
> Karl Green, vocals, guitar
> Alan Wrigley, bass
> Steve Titerington, drums
> Peter Noone, lead vocals

Peter Noone, whose full name was Peter Blair Denis Bernard Noone, began performing as a childhood actor on BBC-TV in the early sixties and was even featured on the UK soap opera *Coronation Street*. At the age of fifteen, Noone filled in, as a singer for a group called the Hearbeats. Audiences loved the sound, and Noone was installed as a permanent member.

There are two similar stories regarding how they came up with the name Herman's Hermits. One is that members of the group told Peter he reminded them of Sherman from the *Rocky and Bullwinkle* cartoon show. They dropped the *S*, and he became Herman. The other story is from an interview I did with Peter many years ago. At that time, Peter said his uncle misheard the name from that same cartoon show and said he resembled Herman. Either way, the name stuck, and Herman's Hermits is now a huge part of pop music history.

It's worth noting that after one hit on the UK charts, Herman's Hermits were never that big in England, but they were a major part of what is known as the British Invasion here in America. The group appeared on popular TV shows in America, such as *The Ed Sullivan Show*, *The Jackie Gleason Show*, and *The Dean Martin Show*. They were far more popular in the US than the UK.

Some of my favorite Herman's Hermits songs
> '64: "I'm into Something Good"
> '65: "Can't You Hear My Heartbeat"
> '65: "Silhouettes"
> '65: "Mrs. Brown, You've Got a Lovely Daughter"

'65: "I'm Henry the Eighth, I Am"
'66: "Dandy"
'67: "There's a Kind of Hush"

THE HOLLIES

Original members
    Allan Clarke
    Graham Nash
    Vic Steele, lead guitar
    Eric Haydock, bass
    Don Rathbone, drums

The Hollies were one of the most successful bands in the UK during the sixties and early seventies. They were originally the skiffle duo of Allan Clark and Graham Nash. At one point, they changed their name to Rick and Dane Young. Soon after, they teamed up with another band called the Fourtones. After a number of personnel changes, Clark and Nash joined a group called the Deltas in the early sixties. It should be noted that of those members that left many went on to success with Freddie and the Dreamers and the Mindbenders.

Prior to a performance in Manchester, England, the Delta's changed their name to the Hollies. It is said that one of the members thought it would be a good name since it was the Christmas season and hollies were a holiday plant. Others say the group thought highly of Buddy *Holly* and the Crickets and used the Hollies as a tribute. Many contend there is a hint of truth to both stories.

Also an interesting note: The Beatles give Buddy Holly and the Crickets some credit for their name as well. See "The Beatles."

In 1968, Graham Nash left the group to form Crosby, Stills, Nash, and Young and was replaced by Terry Sylvester.

Some of my favorite Hollies songs
    '65: "Look through Any Window"
    '66: "Bus Stop"
    '67: "On a Carousel"
    '67: "Carrie Ann"
    '67: Just One Look

'69: "He Ain't Heavy, He's My Brother"
'72: "Long Cool Woman"
'74: "The Air that I Breathe"

HONDELLS

Original members (a group of studio musicians)
    Richard Burns
    Glen Campbell (yes, that Glen Campbell)
    Al DeLory
    Tommy Tedesco
    Richie Podolor

This group was part of the American Surf Sound of the early sixties. They were a studio group led by singer Richard Burns who actually sang in high school in New York before traveling to California to explore the surf sound he was looking for. The Hondells were formed by Mick Curb in order to record a commercial for Honda motorbikes. The commercial was a huge success with the famous line "You meet the nicest people on a Honda."

Following the commercial, the Hondells recorded their big hit "Little Honda" written and recorded by Brian Wilson and Mike Love of the Beach Boys. How many times did the song "Little Honda" play on the radio? Did the Honda company pay a dime to any of those stations for playing what amounted to a two-minute commercial. I think not! Just sayin'! Brilliant strategy by Honda!

My favorite Hondells song
    '64: "Little Honda"

HONEYCOMBS

Original members
    Denis D'Ell, vocals and harmonica
    Martin Murray, rhythm guitar
    Peter Pye (replaced Murray in 1964)
    Allan Ward, guitar
    John Lantree, bass
    Honey Lantree, vocals, drums

This group started as the Sherabons in London, England, in 1963 and featured rock music's only female drummer (at that time) Ann "Honey" Lantree. The Honeycombs took their name from their drummer, Honey, her middle name, and from the fact that she was also a hairdresser at the time Combs (sorta makes sense).

The group's first song "Have I the Right" became a top 5 hit in the US, but that was about all she wrote in America. They did have several other hits in the UK, but their producer passed away, and that was about the end for the Honeycombs.

My favorite Honeycombs song
    '64: "Have I the Right"

HOT TUNA

Original members
    Jorma Kaukonen, vocals, guitar
    Jack Casady, bass
    A number of other musicians that came and went

Hot Tuna was formed from the group Jefferson Airplane around 1970. It was an offshoot of the group developed while Gracie Slick recovered from throat surgery. The only interesting thing about the group (from my perspective) is they originally titled the group Hot Shit, but RCA records put a stop to that. The new name apparently came from someone nicknamed Witty Wag who said "What's that smell, like fish, oh baby" (I won't even try to go where my mind is on that one). It's a line from the song "Keep on Truckin'."

My favorite Hot Tuna songs
    Gotta be honest here: don't have any!

HUES CORPORATION

Original members
  Wally Holmes
  Bernard St. Clair
  H. Ann Kelley

The Hues Corporation was a vocal trio featuring two guys and a girl and a disco-soul sound. Their one big hit was "Rock the Boat," which did hit number 1 in 1974 and sold over two million copies.

The group's original name was actually the Children of Howard Hughes, but their record label said "Ahh, no." According to one source, they changed the name to the Hues Corporation and spelled Hues differently so there would be no legal trouble. Another thought was that they used the name Hues to refer to color.

My favorite Hues Corporation song
  '74: "Rock the Boat"

Humble Pie

Original members
    Steve Marriott, vocals, guitar
    Peter Frampton, vocals, guitar
    Greg Ridley, bass
    Jerry Shirley, drums

Humble Pie was an interesting group formed in Essex, England, in the late sixties. There was great interest from the outset because all the members came from successful groups prior to their initiation: Steve Marriott from Small Faces, Peter Frampton from the Herd, Greg Ridley from Spooky Tooth, and Jerry Shirley from the Apostolic.

Apparently the group just decided to pick Humble Pie for their name. The term is similar to the American phrase "eating crow," which basically means realizing that you have done something terribly wrong and eating crow is the humiliation you get from that recognition.

As for the inclusion in this exercise: I just got a kick out of the names of all the groups these guys came from as well as name Humble Pie.

As for my favorite Humble Pie songs
    They were basically an album-oriented rock group rather than singles

THE IDES OF MARCH

Original members
    James Peterik, vocals, guitar, keyboard
    Ray Herr, vocals, guitar, bass
    Lawrence Millas, guitar, organ
    Robert Bergland, bass, saxophone
    John Larson, horns
    Chuck Somar, horns
    Michael Borch, drums

This group got together in 1964 in Berwyn, Illinois, a suburb of Chicago. The members had been together as friends since grade school. When they went to high school, they formed a band called the Shon-Dels. They even released a song in 1965 called "Like It or Lump It." (Apparently, *lump it* won out because it didn't go anywhere.)

In 1966, they changed their name to the Ides of March. It was bass player Bob Bergland that suggested the name after he read *Julius Caesar* by Shakespeare in high school. The reference to Shakespeare is from a warning to Julius Caesar that he would be killed. He was killed on March 15 on what is now referred to as the Ides of March. It is considered a bad-luck day (beware the ides of March).

The group was often accused of imitating Blood, Sweat & Tears because they had a total of seven members including brass instruments (a rarity in that day). The truth of the matter is, however, that Ides of March was formed before BS&T. Their first song as the Ides was called "You Wouldn't Listen" (sounds like what my wife tells me), which reached number 7 in Chicago. Their major US claim to fame is "Vehicle," which reached number 2 on Billboard's top 100 in 1970.

Interesting note: A guitar solo was accidentally erased on the recording and was later spliced in from an earlier session to complete the song.

My favorite Ides of March song
    '70: "Vehicle"

IRON BUTTERFLY

Original members
   Doug Ingle, vocals, organ
   Jack Pinney, drums
   Greg Willis bass
   Danny Weis, guitar
   Darryl DeLoach, vocals, tambourine
   Jerry Penrod (replaced Willis in 1966)
   Bruce Morse (replaced Pinney)
   Ron Bushy (replaced Morse)

This American rock group is best known for its hard rock and heavy metal music exemplified with "In-A-Gadda-Da-Vida." That 1968 album remains one of the world's best-selling LPs (over thirty million strong). The title song was seventeen minutes long and featured a drum solo of two and a half minutes. The song was edited from seventeen minutes to under three for play in the US. American radio just did not like playing songs of that length (not enough time for commercials). The actual meaning of "In-A-Gadda-Da-Vida" is "In the Garden of Eden." Iron Butterfly only stayed together until 1971.

There's no great story behind the name Iron Butterfly. It apparently comes from one of the members who liked the fact that it implied "hard and soft" at the same time.

A more interesting story about the group (this is one of my favorite stories) is that they were invited to play at Woodstock in 1969. (If you are offended by inappropriate language, please stop here and go on to the next group.) The story goes that the group was on its way to the event and got stuck at LaGuardia Airport (that is something I have in common with them). They called the promoters saying they would be late and then demanded they be flown by helicopter to the concert. Apparently, they waited for the chopper several different times, but it never showed. Subsequently they received a telegram from the promoters that read, "*For reasons I can't go into*

/ *U*ntil you are here / *C*larifying your situation / *K*nowing you are having problems / *Y*ou will have to find / *O*ther transportation / *U*nless you plan not to come." If you put those letters that are bolded together, you will come up with the real message being sent: "Fuck you." (Hmmm, you think somebody was pissed?)

My favorite song by Iron Butterfly
    '69: "In-A-Gadda-Da-Vida"

IRON MAIDEN

Original members
- Steve Harris, bass
- Paul Day, vocals
- Dennis Wilcock, vocals (replaced Day)
- Dave Murray, guitar
- Bob Sawyer, guitar
- Bruce Dickinson, vocals

This group was formed in England in 1975. Bass player Steve Harris helped put the group together after he left his former group called Smiler. Harris says he took the name Iron Maiden from a novel from Alexandre Dumas called *The Man in the Iron Mask*. It apparently reminded him of an ancient English torture device that consisted of an iron cabinet filled with spikes that could enclose a human on the inside. (Those English folks really know how to have fun!)

Iron Maiden never hit it huge in the US but remained very strong as a hard rock / heavy metal band in the UK. Lead singer Bruce Dickinson was given the fascinating name the Air Raid Siren (that's lovely!).

My favorite Iron Maiden songs
Sorry, they just weren't my cup of tea (or shot of vodka, scotch, or any other such libation).

JAMES GANG

Original members
    Joe Walsh, vocals, guitar
    Tom Kriss, bass
    Jim Fox, drums
    Dale Peters (replaced Kriss)

There were actually a number of groups that used the name James Gang. I decided to write a bit about one of them.

This band was formed in Cleveland, Ohio, in 1966. The group was named the James Gang from its founder and drummer, Jim Fox. The James Gang also featured a future member of the Eagles, Joe Walsh, who was considered by some to be the most talented musician of the group.

One of the reasons I included this group in this endeavor is that in 1968 they opened for Cream at the Grande Ballroom in Detroit. I remember being asked if I wanted to attend the show but declined. Damn, I'll bet it was a good show. No doubt, readers of my age from the Detroit area (if any are left—only kidding!) remember the Grande Ballroom.

Favorite James Gang songs
    Sorry, don't have any! Remember, I didn't go to the concert!

JANIS IAN

Janis Fink was born in New York but lived her younger years in New Jersey. At the age of fifteen, Janis learned to play the guitar and would sing at a variety of local clubs. She was signed to a recording deal in 1966, and her first song was called "Society's Child." The song was very controversial and was banned on radio stations because it dealt with interracial relationships. While still in high school, Janis changed her last name to Ian, which was also her brother's middle name.

"Society's Child" remained banned on most radio stations until Leonard Bernstein (conductor of the New York Philharmonic Orchestra) featured the song on a TV show *Inside Pop: The Rock Revolution*. Radio stations then began playing the song, and it reached number 14 on the Billboard Hot 100. Ian also wrote her autobiography, also called *Society's Child*.

At sixteen years old, Janis met Bill Cosby at a show where she was promoting her song. (Hmm, that could have spelled trouble.) Apparently Cosby spotted Ian sleeping with her head in another woman's lap, and according to her manager, Cosby then suggested she was a lesbian. Allegedly, Cosby attempted to blacklist the singer because she "wasn't suitable family entertainment." (Okay, my mind is whirling around with that one. *She* wasn't suitable!)

Janis didn't have much in the way of hits for another nine years until she came up with her biggest hit "At Seventeen" in 1975. The song was a number 1 hit. Janis has won a number of awards, including two Grammys.

My favorite Janis Ian songs
    '66: "Society's Child"
    '75: "At Seventeen"

JAY AND THE AMERICANS

Original members
  John "Jay" Traynor
  Howard Kane
  Kenny Vance
  Sandy Deanne
  Marty Sanders
  David Black (replaced Traynor and took the name Jay Black)

This group started in 1961 out of New York with John Traynor as lead singer. He took the name Jay, and their producers Leiber and Stoller gave the rest of them the name the Americans.

The band's first hit was in 1962 called "She Cried" with Traynor as lead. After the next couple of songs didn't fare well, Traynor left the group. At that point, Marty Sanders, who played guitar for the Empires, joined the group and invited their vocalist David Black to join as well. David then took the name Jay to preserve the original name Jay and the Americans.

The most memorable songs from the group were "Come a Little Bit Closer," which reached number 3 in 1964 and "Cara Mia," which reached number 4 in 1965.

My favorite Jay and the Americans songs
  '62: "She Cried" (with Jay Traynor)
  '64: "Come a Little Bit Closer"
  '65: "Cara Mia"
  '69: "This Magic Moment"
  '70: "Walking in the Rain"

JEFFERSON AIRPLANE / JEFFERSON STARSHIP

Original members
  Marty Balin, vocals
  Paul Kantner, vocals and guitar
  Grace Slick, vocals (replaced Anderson)
  Jorma Kaukonen, vocals, lead guitar
  Jack Casady, bass
  Spencer Dryden, drums
  Signe Anderson, vocals

Jefferson Airplane started in 1965 in San Francisco during the Haight-Ashbury hippie movement (older Detroit area readers will remember Plum Street). The group's vocalists were Signe Anderson, Marty Balin, Paul Kantner, and Jornma Kaukonen. Airplane's sound was part of the San Francisco sound and psychedelic rock.

RCA Records signed the group to a contract, and their first album was called *Jefferson Airplane Takes Off*. Before the album came out, lead singer Signe Anderson left the group because she was having a baby. Grace Slick, a former model from the band Great Society, took her spot, and Jefferson Airplane indeed took off! Slick had a much stronger voice and says she tried to imitate the sound of the lead guitar.

The name Jefferson Airplane was explained in a press release in 2007. Guitarist and vocalist Jornma Kaukonen stated, "I had this friend [Steve Talbot] in Berkeley who came up with funny names for people. His name for me was Blind Thomas Jefferson Airplane [for blues pioneer Blind Lemon Jefferson). When the guys were looking for band names and nobody could come up with something, I remember saying, 'You want a silly band name? I got a silly band name for you!'"

According to *Rolling Stone* magazine, two of their songs, "Somebody to Love" and "White Rabbit," are among "The Greatest

500 Songs of All Time." Jefferson Airplane was inducted into the Rock and Roll Hall of Fame in 1996 and was given the Grammy Lifetime Achievement Award in 2016.

In 1972, Jefferson Airplane broke up into two separate groups. Several members put a band together called Hot Tuna, actually originally called Hot Shit (no, I'm not kidding!), and in 1974 other members, including Grace Slick, took the name Jefferson Starship. In 1975, they produced their most successful album, *Red Octopus*, which hit number 1 and sold over two and a half million records.

There are a lot more interesting stories regarding these groups, but it deviates a bit from the overall theme of this endeavor.

Note: See "Hot Tuna."

My favorite Jefferson Airplane / Jefferson Starship songs
    '67: "Somebody to Love"
    '67: "White Rabbit"

Jefferson Starship
    '75: "Miracles"

JETHRO TULL

Original members
  Ian Anderson, vocals, guitar, flute

Many members came and went
  Mick Abrahams, guitar
  Martin Barre, guitar
  John Evan, keyboard
  Dee Palmer, keyboard
  Clive Bunker, drums
  Barriemore Barlow, drums
  Doane Perry, drums
  Glenn Cornick, bass
  Jeffrey Hammond, bass
  John Glascock, bass
  Dave Pegg, bass

Jethro Tull began in 1967 out of Blackpool, England, with a blues/jazz sound and quickly turned into one of the most successful progressive rock bands out of the UK. The group was started by Ian Anderson who sang, played guitar and flute, and even dabbled with the drums. Other members, more or less, came and went through the years.

The group moved to the London area and performed at local clubs. Things did not progress well. One member said, "We were so poor we would have to share a can of soup or stew as an evening meal."

They decided to change their name several times, including Navy Blue, Ian Hendersons, Bag O' Nails, and Candy Coloured Rain, just to get repeat offers. Once, Anderson said he didn't even recognize their name on a local club's poster.

At one point, a booking agent suggested Jethro Tull, the name of an eighteenth-century agriculturist (yeah, I know, makes a lot of sense to me too). After calling themselves Jethro Tull, they received a second booking and decided to keep the name because of that.

My favorite Jethro Tull songs
Sorry, wasn't really my cup of tea, or glass of vodka!

Jimi Hendrix

Johnny Allen Hendrix was born in 1942 in Seattle, Washington. His dad gave him his first guitar when he was eleven. Later that year, he took up the electric guitar. In 1961 Hendrix enlisted in the US Army but was discharged due to an injury while training as a paratrooper.

At this point, Johnny Allen Hendrix took the name of Jimmy James and played backup guitar to headliners like Sam Cooke, B.B. King, Little Richard, Ike and Tina Turner, and Wilson Picket (apparently those stars recognized his talent). In 1965, Jimi put a band together called Jimmy James and the Blue Flames. A year later, Chas Chandler, who was bass player for the Animals, helped Hendrix put another group together called the Jimi Hendrix Experience.

The Rock and Roll Hall of Fame says Hendrix is "the greatest instrumentalist in the history of rock music." Many consider him to be the most influential guitarist of all time.

Hendrix appeared at Woodstock in 1969 and later formed the Band of Gypsies (an all-black band). Hendrix, at the time, had been pressured to perform before all black audiences with an all-black band.

Jimi Hendrix died in 1970 from an overdose of barbiturates just four years after he became popular.

My favorite Jimi Hendrix songs
  '67: "Purple Haze"
  '67: "Foxy Lady"

JIMMY GILMER AND THE FIREBALLS

Original members
  Jimmy Gilmer, vocals, piano (replaced Tharp)
  George Tomsco, lead guitar
  Chuck Tharp, vocals
  Stan Lark, bass
  Eric Budd, drums
  Dan Trammell, rhythm guitar
  Doug Roberts, drums (replaced Budd)

Jimmy Gilmer and the Fireballs, sometimes just known as the Fireballs, were from Raton, New Mexico, and were popular in the late fifties through about 1965. Jimmy Gilmer, from Amarillo, Texas, ran into the Fireballs at a recording studio in Clovis, New Mexico.

It is said the Fireballs took their name from the Jerry Lee Lewis hit "Great Balls of Fire." The group had their biggest hit and one of the biggest of 1963 with "Sugar Shack." Following that, they also had a couple of minor hits and then Gilmer left the group in 1964.

Gilmer didn't have a great deal of success on his own, but the Fireballs followed up in 1968 with "Bottle of Wine."

Some of my favorite hits from the group
  '63: "Sugar Shack" (Jimmy and the group)
  '68: "Bottle or Wine" (Fireballs only)

JOHN DENVER

Henry John Deutchendorf Jr. was born in Roswell, New Mexico, and was the son of a famous Air Force Pilot Henry John "Dutch" Deutchendorf. His dad is in the Air Force Hall of Fame and holds a number of speed records in a B-58 bomber.

During his early years, he and his family moved many times because of his father's service responsibilities. John (I don't want to type that other name too often, my hands are cramping) received a guitar from his grandmother at the age of eleven and taught himself to play.

While attending college in Texas and after playing in some of the local clubs there, John was heard by Randy Sparks, founder of the New Christy Minstrels. Sparks told him that Deutchendorf wouldn't fit well on posters or marquees. At that point, he decided to change his name to Denver, a tribute to the state he loved so much, Colorado.

Interesting note: In 1967 Denver wrote and recorded a song called "Babe I Hate to Go" and later renamed it "Leaving on a Jet Plane." Denver's producer also was producer for Peter Paul and Mary, and they recorded the song that became a number 1 hit. Denver's version was also a hit in the UK. Denver was also into ecology and campaigned for President Jimmy Carter when he ran against Ronald Reagan.

John Denver won a load of awards over the years. Some of those awards include the following:

- Academy of Country Music Album of the Year 1974 for *Back Home Again*
- American Music Awards: Favorite Pop/Rock Male Artist, 1975
- American Music Awards: Favorite Country Album for *Back Home Again*
- American Music Awards: Favorite Country Male Artist, 1976

- Country Music Association Entertainer of the Year, 1975
- Country Music Association Song of the Year for "Back Home Again"

Denver also won an Emmy and two Grammys and was inducted into the Songwriters Hall of Fame in 1996.

My favorite John Denver songs
'71: "Take Me Home Country Roads"
'73: "Rocky Mountain High"
'74: "Sunshine on My Shoulders"
'74: "Annie's Song"
'75: "Thank God I'm a Country Boy"
'75: "I'm Sorry"
'75: "Calypso"

JONESES

Original members
> Glenn Dorsey
> Harold Taylor
> Cy Brooks
> Ernest Holt

Actually there were a number of bands that called themselves the Joneses. Interestingly, though, this version of the Joneses had no one named Jones in the group. They formed in the late sixties out of Pittsburgh and eventually moved to New York to get into the music business. They had one hit called "Sugar Pie Guy."

Oh, yes, the Joneses came up with the name because they wanted to be the group that all the other groups would have to keep up with, as in the phrase "keep up with the Joneses." I'm guessing it didn't quite work out the way they expected.

My favorite Joneses song
> '74: "Sugar Pie Guy"

JOURNEY

Original members
    Neal Schon, lead guitar
    Gregg Rolie, vocals, keyboards
    Ross Valory, bass
    George Tickner, rhythm guitar
    Prairie Prince, drums

Journey began as a progressive rock group in 1975 and evolved into a hard rock or hard pop band in the late seventies. It is said (by some) that Journey got their name from a radio station contest. Listeners on KSAN-FM in San Francisco were asked to come up with a name for the band. Journey won out and the rest is history. Another story is that picking a name from radio listeners did not go well and one of their roadies by the name of John Villanueva suggested the name.

Journey has sold nearly fifty million albums in the US and over seventy-five million worldwide. An opinion poll from the *USA Today* puts Journey in the top 5 rock bands of all time. They were inducted into the Rock and Roll Hall of Fame in 2017.

My favorite Journey songs
    '80: "Any Way You Want It"
    '81: "Who's Crying Now"
    '96: "When You Love a Woman"

KANSAS

Original members
> Don Montre, guitar
> Robby Steinhardt, vocals, violin
> Steve Walsh, keyboards, vocals
> Kerry Livgren, guitar
> Rich Williams, guitar
> Dave Hope, bass
> Phil Ehart, drums
> Lynn Meredith, vocals
> Dan Wright, vocals
> Scott Kessler, bass
> Zeke Lowe, drums

In 1969, Don Montre and Kerry Livgren began playing in a band in their hometown of Wichita, Kansas, called the Reasons Why. Shortly thereafter, they left that band and started a new band called Saratogo and invited Lynn Meredith, Dan Wright, Scott Kessler, and Zeke Lowe to join the effort.

In 1970, they merged with a group called White Clover. At this point, Dave Hope and Phil Ehart joined, and they changed their name to Kansas. Since they all lived in the state, it was a move that made sense. Over the years, Kansas went through a number of personnel changes with as many as fifteen different members.

Kansas was inducted into the Rock Walk Hall of Fame in 1995. (Being honest, which I am occasionally, it's the first time I've ever heard of that, but after research, it's pretty big in Hollywood, California.)

My favorite Kansas song
> '78: "Dust in the Wind"

KC AND THE SUNSHINE BAND

Original members
Harry Wayne Casey (KC)
Richard Finch
Jerome Smith, guitar
Robert Johnson, drums

The group started in Hialeah, Florida, in 1973. They were best known for their funky dance music called, by some, the Miami sound and were considered among the best in that genre. Howard Wayne Casey and Richard Finch met each other working at a company called Tone Distributors and eventually started writing music together. Soon after putting their heads together they formed a band called KC and the Junkanoo Band. (To be totally honest, my research became the first time I ever heard of junkanoo!) Junkanoo features a lot of drums, horns, whistles, and vocals that originated in the Bahamas.

After their first record, called "Blow Your Whistle," they dropped Junkanoo from their name. The rest of the name came from Howard's last name (even though it starts with a *C* not a *K*) and the fact that they came from Florida, the Sunshine State. So KC and the Sunshine Band was born. To record their songs, they used a local junkanoo band called the Miami Junkanoo Band and some other local musicians from a place called T.K. Studios.

My favorite KC and the Sunshine Band songs
'75: "Get Down Tonight"
'75: "That's the Way (I Like It)"
'76: "Shake Your Booty (Shake Shake Shake)"
'78: "It's the Same Old Song"

KEITH

James Barry Keefer grew up in Philadelphia, Pennsylvania, and decided singing would be his career. He also decided that James Barry Keefer would not work and came up with Keith because he saw the success of Donovan using a one-word name. It didn't work as well for Keith. However, he did have a hit with the song "98.6."

My favorite Keith song
'66: "98.6"

KINKS

Original members
    Ray Davies, vocals, guitar, keyboards
    Dave Davies, vocals, lead guitar
    Mick Avory, drums
    Pete Quaife, bass
    Nicky Hopkins, keyboard

This group was formed in 1963 in a suburb of London, England, by brothers Ray and Dave Davies. After including some high school buddies, they became the Ray Davies Quintet. The group used a number of different lead singers, including Rod Stewart, for a brief time, who went to school with them. After some other personnel changes, they took the name the Ray Davies Quartet then the Ramrods and eventually the Ravens.

In 1964, they decided they needed another name change. One story suggested they "needed a gimmick, some edge, to get attention." Here it was: kinkiness—something newsy, naughty, but just on the borderline of acceptability.

Manager Robert Wace said, "I had a friend… He thought the group was rather fun. If my memory is correct, he came up with the name just as an idea, as a good way of getting publicity. When they approached the band members with the idea, they said, 'No way! We don't want to be known as kinky.'" Ray Davies said another guy suggested the name because of the kinky clothes the guys wear. Whatever the story, the name stuck! And with great success! In their heyday, in the middle of the British Invasion, the Kinks were one of the best rock bands of the sixties.

Some of my favorite Kinks songs
    '64: "You Really Got Me"
    '64: "All Day and All of the Night"
    '65: "Tired of Waiting for You"
    '65: "A Well Respected Man"

KISS

Original members
    Paul Stanley
    Gene Simmons
    Peter Criss
    Ace Frehley

Kiss is probably known most prominently as "the band without a face." Kiss started in New York in 1973 and featured a bunch of evil cartoon characters. It is said their real faces had never been photographed, but that was debunked when they performed without their makeup later in their career.

Gene Simmons is probably the most well-known and most bizarre member of Kiss. He performed as the Demon, a fire-breathing, blood-spewing, tongue-lashing ghoul. Prior to Kiss, Simmons was a public school teacher in New York City. (What!)

Paul Stanley of the group actually came up with the name Kiss as he, Gene Simmons, and Peter Criss were touring New York. After Criss said he had been in the band Lips, Stanley said, "What about Kiss?" They all liked the idea, and the rest is history. Another member, Ace Frehley, designed the logo, making the *SS* in Kiss look like lightning bolts: KI⚡⚡. But that became a problem! The ⚡⚡ in the logo looked very similar to the *SS* in the Nazi symbol in World War II. To be honest, Gene Simmons and Paul Stanley both deny any linkage to Nazis since both of them are Jewish. But while performing in Germany or Israel or a number of other countries, the group used *S*'s that look like backward *Z*'s **KISS** instead of lightning bolts.

There were also a number of rumors that the name was an acronym for Kids in Satan's Service and Knights in Satan's Service. That might have been great for publicity for their style of music but untrue, according to Gene Simmons.

To be sure, Kiss is one of the greatest-selling bands of all time with more than seventy-five million records and twenty-five million albums sold worldwide. In 2014, Kiss was inducted into the Rock and Roll Hall of Fame and is considered one of the greatest hard rock bands of all time.

My favorite Kiss songs
'74: "Kissin' Time"
'75: "Rock & Roll All Night"
'76: "Beth/Detroit Rock City"

KNICKERBOCKERS

Original members
　　Beau Charles, vocals, guitar
　　John Charles, vocals, bass
　　Buddy Randell, vocals, sax
　　Jimmy Walker, drums

These guys formed in 1964 as the Castle Kings and then changed their name to the Knickerbockers, which is the name of one of the streets in their hometown of Bergenfield, New Jersey. I also wonder if they were basketball fans of the New York Knicks, who were also known as the Knickerbockers when they started in 1946. The name also refers to Dutch colonists that settled in the New York area in the 1700s.

The Knickerbockers only had one viable hit, which was in 1965 called "Lies" and was a Beatles soundalike. They almost had another hit with "One Track Mind," but their record company fell short with distribution, and the song only made it into the top 50.

One of the highlights for the Knickerbockers was a number of appearances on ABC's *Where the Action Is.*

My favorite Knickerbockers tune
　　'65: "Lies"

KOOL & THE GANG

Original members
    Robert "Kool" Bell
    Ronald Bell
    Dennis "DT" Thomas
    Robert "Spike" Mickens
    Charles Smith
    George Brown
    Ricky West

This group formed in 1964 when some school friends from Lincoln High in Jersey City, New Jersey, got together and started a soul/jazz band called the Jazziacs. The leader of the group was Robert "Kool" Bell, who played bass.

The group moved from the Jazziacs to the Soul Town Band and then the New Dimensions while they concentrated on the newly arising Motown sound. In 1967, the group changed their name again to Kool & the Flames but decided, with advice from their manager, to change again because it was too close to James Brown's band the Famous Flames. In 1969, they changed their name to Kool & the Gang. Obviously the Kool part came from their leader Robert "Kool" Bell, who used the *kool* part to be "cool" with the gangs in his neighborhood.

An interesting note: Bell's father, Bobby, and his uncle Tommy moved to New York to train as boxers. None other than jazz great Miles Davis would come around to their apartment because he also wanted to be a boxer.

My favorite Kool & the Gang songs
    '69: "The Gang's Back Again"
    '70: "Funky Town"
    '80: "Celebration"

THE LEAVES

Original members
> William Rinehart, vocals
> John Beck, guitar
> Robert Lee Teiner, guitar
> James Pons, bass
> Tom "Ambrose" Ray, drums

The Leaves took their name from a conversation between members. One of them said, "What's happening?" and the response was, "The leaves are happening." Apparently, they were watching leaves fall from a nearby tree.

The group was put together by Robert Reiner and Jim Pons at Cal State in LA. They were fraternity brothers and originally called themselves the Rockwells.

My favorite Leaves song
> '66: "Hey Joe"

LED ZEPPELIN

Original members
    Robert Plant, vocals guitar
    Jimmy Page, guitar
    John Paul Jones, bass, keyboard
    John Bonham, drums

This group formed in London, England, in 1966 and were known as the Yardbirds. In 1968, the group was scheduled for a Scandinavian tour but was faced with a number of changes in the group's personnel and essentially broke up. At that point, members including Robert Plant and Jimmy Page and former members, agreed that they could form under the name the New Yardbirds.

After their Scandinavian tour, the New Yardbirds recorded an album based on their recent live performances but then were given legal information they could only use their new name for that single tour. Two former members of the group suggested that whatever name was chosen, the group would go down like a "lead balloon." Keith Moon of the Who (a good friend of Page) suggested Lead Zeppelin as a replacement for lead balloon. Plant and Page liked it then decided it could be a good way to rub it in (so to speak). They also decided to take the *a* out of *lead*. At that point, Led Zeppelin was born.

Led Zeppelin was inducted into the Rock and Roll Hall of Fame in 1995 and were considered "the heaviest band of all time" according to *Rolling Stone* magazine. It's estimated they have sold between two to three hundred million records overall.

My favorite Led Zeppelin songs
    '69: "Whole Lotta Love"
    '71: "Black Dog"
    '72: "Rock & Roll"

LEFT BANKE

Original members
    Steven Martin, lead vocals
    Jeff Winfield, lead guitar
    Michael Brown, keyboards
    Tomas Finn, bass
    George Cameron, drums

The Left Banke got together in 1965 in New York City. Michael Brown's father, Harry Lookofsky, became the band's producer and manager and, just as important, had his own recording studio. (Big help there.)

In 1966, the group released "Walk Away Renee." The song sold slowly at first then became a local hit in Ohio but held on and became a top 10 hit. The group followed up with another hit called "Pretty Ballerina" the following year.

As for the name Left Banke; apparently Martin and Brown had dinner with songwriter Scott English one day and he thought of the name. The group liked it and decided to add an *e* at the end of bank to make the name special.

Interesting note: "Walk Away Renee" is considered to be one of the 500 Greatest Songs of All Time according to *Rolling Stone* magazine.

My favorite Left Banke songs
    '66: "Walk Away Renee"
    '67: "Pretty Ballerina"

LEO SAYER

Gerard Hugh Sayer first performed in the early seventies with a band from Sussex, England, called Terraplane Blues. He followed that by joining a new band called Patches. The group recorded one single and sold fifty-five records (not what you would call an enormous hit). In 1973, Sayer began writing songs for British singer Adam Faith. At that point, Sayer began a solo career. It was Adam's wife, Jackie, that suggested Sayer use the name Leo, because she thought he looked like a lion. And Leo Sayer was born.

Sayer had a number of hits as a solo artist including "Long Tall Glasses" and "You Make Me Feel Like Dancing." He also wrote several songs for other groups like the Who and Three Dog Night.

Interesting note: At the age of eighteen, Sayer helped rescue a number of elderly people from a hotel that caught on fire.

My favorite Leo Sayer Songs
    '75: "Long Tall Glasses"
    '76: "You Make Me Feel Like Dancing"
    '77: "When I Need You"
    '77: "Easy to Love"

LIGHTHOUSE

Original members
>Skip Prokop, vocals, drums
>Paul Hoffert, keyboard
>Ralph Coles, guitar
>Plus studio session musicians to a total of up to thirteen members

This group started in 1968 out of Toronto, Ontario, Canada, eh! Initially the band was formed by Skip Prokop (vocalist and drummer) and Paul Hoffert (keyboard). Eventually the band had thirteen members and featured rock, jazz, swing, and a bit of classical music. Lighthouse won a number of awards in Canada, including Best Canadian Group of the Year in '72, '73, and '74. Prokop also brought in Ralph Cole as lead guitarist when he saw him perform in Detroit at the Grande Ballroom (I like making reference to my hometown whenever possible).

The name Lighthouse was the idea of Skip Prokop, who, at one point, stared at an aquarium and saw a number of fish swimming out of a lighthouse. They did achieve some US success with "One Fine Morning."

My favorite Lighthouse song
>'71: "One Fine Morning"

LITTLE RIVER BAND

Original members
  Beeb Birtles, vocals, guitar
  Ric Formosa, vocals
  Graeham Goble, vocals, guitar
  Roger McLachian, vocals
  Derek Pellicci, drums
  Glenn Shorrock, lead vocals
  David Briggs (replaced Formosa)

This group started in 1975 out of Melbourne, Australia. The band went through many personnel changes over the years. After the group got together, they called themselves Mississippi (hmmmm, a group from Australia calling themselves Mississippi).

Anyway, they also performed under the name Drummond.

Mississippi/Drummond had several hits in Australia and tried their efforts in the United Kingdom but got mixed reviews. They also performed in the US (without much success) before going back to Melbourne, Australia. At this point, the group talked about a name change. On the way to perform in a concert, they drove by a road sign that said Little River. One of the members of the band shouted out from the back and said "How about Little River Band?" and the rest is history.

Little River Band received numerous awards. Their song "Cool Change" was considered one of the top thirty Australian songs of all time, and they had ten singles that reached the Billboard top 20 in the seventies here in the US.

My favorite Little River Band songs
  '77: "I'll Always Call Your Name"
  '77: "Help Is on the Way"
  '79: "Lady"

LOBO

Lobo is not a group (as is often thought) but the stage name of Kent LaVoie from Winter Haven, Florida. LaVoie was a member of several bands through the sixties like the Rumours, Sugar Beats, US Male, the Uglies, and Me and the Other Guys (how did he remember them all?).

In 1971, LaVoie decided he needed a stage name and started calling himself Lobo, which is Spanish for "wolf." In that same year, he recorded his biggest hit, "Me and You and a Dog Named Boo" (maybe Boo was a wolf!).

My favorite Lobo songs
'71: "Me and You and a Dog Named Boo"
'72: "I'd Love You to Want Me"
'72: "Don't Expect Me to Be Your Friend"

LOU CHRISTIE

He was born, Lugee Alfredo Giovanni Sacco in 1943. Sacco was given a scholarship to attend Moon Area High School, where he studied music and formed a group called the Classics. In 1958, he met a thirty-five-year-old woman musician, Twyla Herbert (twenty years older, hmmmm), who wound up singing and writing songs with him. Twyla also claimed to be a medium and predicted Sacco's success. Sacco sang with another group called Lugee & the Lions and released a few records on a local Pittsburgh label.

At that point, Sacco approached record producer Nick Cenci, who took him under his wing. Cenci suggested Sacco should listen to some other falsetto-style singers like Frankie Vali and Del Shannon.

In 1962, Sacco recorded the "The Gypsy Cried," a song cowritten by him and his friend Twyla. Cenci liked the song and released it under the name Lou Christie. An interesting twist is that Sacco didn't realize his name had been changed until his saw the record. Fortunately, Sacco kind of liked the new name and said his dad would like the change because it contained the name Christ in it.

My favorite Lou Christie songs
    '62: "The Gypsy Cried"
    '62: "Two Faces Have I"
    '63: "Stay"
    '65: "A Teenager in Love"
    '65: "Lightning Strikes"

THE LOVIN' SPOONFUL

(Also see 10cc)

Original members
   John Benson Sebastian, lead vocals
   Zalman Yanovsky, lead guitar
   John Stephen Boon, bass
   Joseph Campbell Butler, drums

John and Zal were members of a group that featured Mama Cass Elliot and Denny Doherty called the Mugwumps. After Mama and Denny left to form the Mamas and Papas, John and Zal started their group called Lovin Spoonful. That name is said to be taken from a song by Mississippi John Hurt, a blues singer from (you guessed it) Mississippi. However, a more interesting version is the same story in which 10cc got their name. See "10cc," and you'll understand what I mean.

My favorite Lovin' Spoonful songs
   '65: "Do You Believe in Magic"
   '65: "You Didn't Have to be so Nice"
   '66: "Did You Ever Have to Make Up Your Mind?"
   '66: "Summer in the City"
   '66: "Nashville Cats"

LYNYRD SKYNYRD

Original members
    Ronald Van Zant, lead vocals
    Ed King, vocals, rhythm guitar
    Allen Collins, vocals, rhythm guitar
    Gary Rossington, vocals, rhythm guitar
    Leon Wilkeson, bass
    William Powell, keyboards
    Robert Burns, drums
    Larry Junstrom, bass

Van Zant, Burns, and Rossington were high school buddies in Jacksonville, Florida. One day they met at Burns's parents' house with their instruments and decided to play their version of "Time Is on My Side" from the Rolling Stones. They liked how they sounded together and decided to form a band. They added Allen Collins and Larry Junstrom to the group and called themselves My Backyard, then the Nobel Five, and then One Percent.

In 1969, Van Zant decided they needed a new name because members of the audience started to shout out that their level of talent was about 1 percent. Burns then suggested they use the name Leonard Skinnerd to mock their old high school physical ed. Teacher, a man whose name was Leonard Skinner. Apparently, Skinner criticized the boys in his class if they had long hair. The group also decided to use an imaginative spelling of the name, and they became Lynyrd Skynyrd. (I'm sorry, but I have to say this! What a bunch of whiners! Back in my day, we got hassled if our tie wasn't on straight.)

Interesting note: The group actually became friendly with their PE teacher and asked him to introduce them at a concert in Jacksonville.

My favorite Lynyrd Skynyrd songs
    '74: "Sweet Home Alabama"
    '74: "Free Bird"
    '77: "What's Your Name"

MAIN INGREDIENT

Original members
    Donald McPherson
    Luther Simmons Jr.
    Tony Silvester
    Cuba Gooding Sr. (replaced McPherson, who died of leukemia
in 1971)

This group began in 1964 as a trio and started with the name Poets then changed it to the Insiders and finally to the Main Ingredient. McPherson, Simmons Jr., and Silvester were the original members, but the most influential member was Cuba Gooding Sr., who replaced McPherson when he unexpectedly died of leukemia. The group took the name when one of the members read it on a bottle of Coke.

Interesting note: Cuba Gooding Sr. also had a story about his name. His father, Dudley Gooding, fled from his native Barbados in 1936 to Cuba and married a woman there named Addie Alston. She was murdered in Cuba because of a political affiliation. Dudley promised his wife before she died that he would name their son Cuba. Cuba Gooding Sr. stayed the course and named his son Cuba Gooding Jr., who is an actor and played in the movie *Jerry McGuire* with Tom Cruise.

My favorite Main Ingredient song
    '72: "Everybody Plays the Fool"

THE MAMAS & THE PAPAS

Original members
John Phillips
Michelle Phillips
Denny Doherty
Cass Elliot

John and Michelle Phillips were husband and wife and members of the New Journeymen in 1964. Denny Doherty was a member of the Mugwumps. Those three decided to start a group, and Doherty asked Cass Elliot to join. John Phillips was not totally on board with the idea because Elliot was so heavy and might be a detriment to the group. Finally he agreed, and the group was complete. At first, they decided on the name the Magic Cyrcle but switched to the Mamas & Papas because the motorcycle group Hells Angels female members were called mamas (now that's a good reason!).

The Mamas & Papas had over a dozen hits from 1964 to 1968 until they began to break up. "Monday, Monday" became a number 1 hit in the US and won a Grammy in 1967. The group was inducted into the Rock and Roll Hall of Fame in 1998.

My favorite Mamas and Papas songs
'66: "California Dreaming"
'66: "Monday, Monday"
'66: "I Saw Her Again"
'66: "Words of Love"
'67: "Dedicated to the One I Love"
'67: "Creeque Alley"
'68: "Do You Wanna Dance"

MANFRED MANN &
MANFRED MANN'S
EARTH BAND

Original members
  Mick Rogers, lead vocals, guitar
  Manfred Mann, keyboards, synthesizer
  Colin Pattenden, bass
  Chris Slade, drums
  Paul Jones, lead vocals, '62–'66
  Mike d'Abo, lead vocals, '66–'69

This group began as just Manfred Mann and then the Mann-Hugg Blues Brothers in 1963. Their biggest hit was "Do Wah Diddy Diddy." In '71, the group took the name of their keyboard player, Manfred Mann (again), and added Earth Band. One former member of the band, Klaus Voormann, says he came up with the name Earth Band because he felt the group should be more "earthier and rockier." Apparently, according to Voormann, the band had an "effeminate" image, and it caused some difficult encounters in Ireland. However, the official version is that the name came from their drummer, Chris Slade, and according to him, it was due to ecological incentives.

My favorite Manfred Mann and Manfred Mann's Earth Band songs
  '64: "Do Wah Diddy Diddy" (Manfred Mann)
  '64: "Sha La La" (Manfred Mann)
  '68: "The Mighty Quinn" (Manfred Mann)
  '76: "Blinded by the Light" (Manfred Mann's Earth Band)

MARSHALL TUCKER BAND

Original members
   Doug Gray, lead vocals, percussion
   Toy Caldwell, lead guitar
   George McCorkle, rhythm guitar
   Jerry Eubanks, sax, flute, percussion
   Tommy Caldwell, bass
   Paul Riddle, drums

This group began in early sixties in South Carolina as the Toy Factory named after their lead guitarist and prolific songwriter Toy Caldwell. In 1968, the group broke up because a number of members of the group were drafted into the Armed Services due to the war in Vietnam. Caldwell was actually wounded there.

The origin of Marshall Tucker band is a little bizarre. In 1970, the band rented an old warehouse in Spartanburg, South Carolina, to work on their music. One of the guys spotted a key in the warehouse door with the name Marshall Tucker on it. At that point, they put their collective heads together and must have figured it was an omen, and they became the Marshall Tucker Band. Interesting note: The actual Marshall Tucker was not the owner of the building but a blind piano tuner who previously had rented the warehouse.

My favorite Marshall Tucker Band songs
   '77: "Heard It in a Love Song"
   '77: "Can't You See"

McCoys

Original members

Richard Zehringer (later known as Rick Derringer), lead vocals, guitar

Randy Zehringer (later known as Randy Z), drums

Dennis Kelly, drums

Randy Jo Hobbs, bass

Sean Michaels, sax

Ronnie Brandon, keyboards

Originally this trio was known as the Rick Z Combo, then later as Rick and the Raiders. Soon after, Kelly, their drummer, left the group, and Randy Jo Hobbs joined as bass player, Sean Michaels playing sax, and Ronnie Brandon on keyboards all joined.

The band toyed with another name and took a song from the Ventures called McCoy as their new moniker. The McCoys are best known for their number 1 hit song "Hang on Sloopy." The song is the official rock song, of the State of Ohio and the unofficial fight song of Ohio State University. (Hmmm, I wonder if they know how to spell *Sloopy*? Sorry, I'm from Michigan. I had to stick that in.)

My favorite McCoys songs

'65: "Hang on Sloopy"

'65: "Fever"

Meat Loaf

Marvin Lee Aday was born on September 27, 1947, in Dallas, Texas. He is known not only as a singer but a proficient actor. He came up with the name Meat Loaf because his parents were embarrassed about his being a singer and didn't want his real name used. At 6 feet, 2 inches and 260 pounds (that might be an underestimate), the name seems to fit.

There are several interesting stories regarding Meat Loaf. In the mid-seventies, he joined forces with songwriter Jim Steinman. That proved to be a huge benefit. Steinman wrote the material for his first album called *Bat Out of Hell.* He followed that with two additional albums, *Bat Out of Hell II* and *Bat Out of Hell III.* Sales of those three LPs total more than 50 million and continue to sell nearly 200,000 copies a year.

Meat Loaf has also appeared in dozens of movies and TV shows. His movie credits include *The Rocky Horror Picture Show* and *Fight Club*, and he appeared in the musical *Hair* on Broadway. (For those readers who might not remember, actors appeared nude in hair. Remember, Meat Loaf is 6 feet, 2 inches, and over 260 pounds. Now try to get that picture out of your mind.)

Another note of interest: On November 22, 1963, Meat Loaf along with a buddy, and his buddy's dad went to Love Field Airport outside of Dallas to see President John F. Kennedy land there. On the way back, they heard on the radio that Kennedy had been shot. They then drove to the hospital where they saw Texas Governor John Connally getting taken out of the car along with Jackie Kennedy. The president had apparently already been taken out.

My favorite Meat Loaf song
    '78: "Two Out of Three Ain't Bad"

MITCH RYDER AND THE DETROIT WHEELS

Original members
  Mitch Ryder (William S. Levise), lead vocals
  James McCarty, lead guitar
  Joseph Kubert, rhythm guitar
  Earl Elliott, bass
  "Little" John Badanjek, drums

In the early sixties, William Levise started his musical career by forming a band in high school called the Tempest, followed by another band called the Peps. Sometime later in the midsixties, he started singing in a club in Detroit called the Village, where he met McCarty, Elliot, and Badanjek. Levise, then organized a new group with those three called Billy Lee and the Rivieras.

In 1965, the group began recording and getting airplay on several local radio stations. One of those stations, WXYZ in Detroit, featured a well-known disc jockey Bob Prince. He promoted the band to a New York record producer by the name of Bob Crewe. Crewe was impressed and signed them to a contract. However, he realized there was another group that already used the name the Rivieras and decided this new group needed a new name. After looking in the New York phone book, he came up with Mitch Ryder. Then due to the group coming from Detroit, he suggested the Detroit Wheels. At that point, William Levise became Mitch Ryder, and the backup band, the Detroit Wheels.

Soon after getting the group together with their new name they had their first big hit, "Jenny Take a Ride." The song reached number 10 on the national charts and number 1 on the R & B charts. Interesting note: Crewe originally chose the song to be the B-side of their record, but changed his mind when two members of the Rolling Stones, Brian Jones and Keith Richards, who were there during the recording session both loved the song and the group's style.

HOW THE HECK DID THEY GET THOSE NAMES?   141

One year later, Mitch Ryder and the Detroit Wheels hit again with "Little Latin Lupe Lu" and again with a medley called "Devil with the Blue Dress On / Good Golly Miss Molly."

My favorite Mitch Ryder and the Detroit Wheels songs
'65: "Jenny Take a Ride"
'66: "Little Latin Lupe Lu"
'66: "Devil with the Blue Dress on / Good Golly Miss Molly"
'67: "Too Many Fish in the Sea"
'67: "Sock It to Me, Baby"

MONKEES

Original members
 Mickey Dolenz, lead vocals, guitar, drums
 Peter Tork, vocals, guitar
 Michael Nesmith, vocals, bass
 Davy Jones, vocals, tambourine

The idea for the Monkees actually came in 1962 from Bob Rafelson, a filmmaker, who wanted to sell the idea of a TV show to Universal Pictures. The idea was rejected. Rafelson then teamed up with a man named Bert Schneider whose father was CEO of Screen Gems, the TV division of Columbia Pictures. Rafelson says the Beatles film *A Hard Day's Night* inspired him and Schneider to present the idea again, this time to Screen Gems. Now they needed to find a group to be the Monkees.

They originally tried to get the Lovin Spoonful to become the group, but they turned the idea down. At this point, they decided to hold auditions and ran this ad in the *Hollywood Reporter*:

> *Madness!! Auditions. Folk & Roll Musicians-*
> *Singers for acting roles in new TV series. Running*
> *Parts for 4 insane boys, age 17–21. Want spirited*
> *Ben Frank's types. Have courage to work. Must come*
> *down for interview.*

They got over four hundred auditions and chose Tork, Dolenz, and Nesmith. The other role went to Davy Jones before the auditions took place because they liked the fact that he was nominated for a Tony Award for his role in the Broadway show *Oliver* and had loads of experience in TV and movie roles.

Interesting note: During the initial stages of the TV show, the Monkees did not play any instruments and only sang. Studio musicians handled the instruments.

Eventually they began to supervise their sessions, and all became notable as actors and musicians. Note the misspelling of the word Monkees, just like the Beatles and the Byrds.

The Monkees were incredibly popular both with their music and their TV show during the mid- to late sixties. They even had a comic book from *Dell Comics* from 1967 to 1969.

My favorite Monkees songs
'66: "Last Train to Clarksville"
'66: "I'm a Believer"
'66: "Stepping Stone"
'67: "Little Bit Me, a Little Bit You"
'67: "Pleasant Valley Sunday"
'67: "Words"
'67: "Daydream Believer"
'68: "Valleri"
'68: "It's Nice to Be with You"

MOODY BLUES

Original members
> Denny Laine, lead vocals
> Justin Hayward, lead vocals (replaced Laine)
> Ray Thomas, sax, flute
> Michael Pinder, keyboards
> Clint Warwick, bass
> John Lodge, bass (replaced Warwick)
> Graeme Edge, drums

This group got together in Birmingham, England, in 1964. Thomas, Lodge, and Pinder were originally members of El Riot & the Rebels then became the Krew Cats. At this point, Michael Pinter and Ray Thomas recruited Clint Warwick as their bass player because John Lodge was still in college.

They needed a new name and tried to get the Mitchells & Butlers Brewery to sponsor them. They were then calling themselves the M-Bs or the M-B Five in hopes of getting the brewing company's support. That didn't work out, and they changed their name to the Moody Blues. According to band members, it was Mike Pinder who came up with the name because their music helped change people's moods and they played a lot of blues at the time.

The Moody Blues are members of the Vocal Group Hall of Fame and the Rock and Roll Hall of Fame.

My favorite Moody Blues songs
> '65: "Go Now"
> '66: "Stop"
> '68: "Tuesday Afternoon"
> '72: "Nights in White Satin"

MUNGO JERRY

Original members
> Ray Dorset, lead vocals, guitar
> Colin Earl, keyboards
> Michael Cole, bass
> Paul King, acoustic guitar
> David Bidwell, drums

This British group was originally known as the Good Earth Rock & Roll Band. They played in pubs and small venues in England in the early seventies. After a series of personnel changes, they changed their name to Mungo Jerry. According to most, it was based on a T. S. Eliot poem called "Mungojerrie and Rumpleteazer" (that's the name I thought of—okay, maybe I can use Rumpleteazer).

My favorite Mungo Jerry song
> '70: "In the Summertime"

NASHVILLE TEENS

Original members
> Arthur Sharp, lead vocals
> Peter Shannon, guitar
> John Allen, guitar
> John Hawkens, keyboards
> Raymond Phillips, bass, harmonica

I'll bet everyone is figuring this band started in Nashville, Tennessee, right? Well, that's what I would have thought too, but noooo! In 1962, this group started (in of all places) Weybridge, Surrey, England. Whaaattt?

The group picked the name Nashville Teens because they spent a lot of time backing up American Country Rock stars that toured Europe, most notably Jerry Lee Lewis in Germany. They also backed country star Carl Perkins and Chuck Berry as he toured the UK.

The Nashville Teens did have one big hit on their own called "Tobacco Road," which did very well both in England and the US.

My favorite Nashville Teens song
> 64: Tobacco Road (you guessed it!)

NAZARETH

Original members
Dan McCafferty, lead vocals
Manny Charlton, guitar
Peter Agnew, bass
Daryl Sweet, drums

This group started in 1968 out of Dunfermline, Scotland. Originally they were known as the Shadettes. One might think they took their name from the city in Israel, but nooo! They took their name from an American band called the Band (now there's an original name for a band), who recorded a song called "The Weight." In that song was the line "I pulled into Nazareth, was feelin' about half past dead." And Nazareth was born.

In 1975, Nazareth released their first LP called *Hair of the Dog*, which featured a great old tune called "Son of a Bitch" (can't tell you how many times I've sung that song loud and clear). The LP also included their biggest hit called "Love Hurts."

My favorite Nazareth songs
'75: "Love Hurts"
'75: "Son of a Bitch" (oops, my wife's calling me, maybe she's just singing that song)

NAZZ

Original members
>Todd Rundgren, guitar
>Carson Van Osten, bass
>Thom Mooney, drums
>Robert "Stewkey" Antoni, vocals, and keyboard

This group started in 1967 in Philadelphia. Todd Rundgren left his original group called Woody's Truckstop to start his own band with his bass player Carson Van Osten. Then Mooney and Antoni joined the effort.

The group chose the Nazz from a Yardbirds song called the Nazz Are Blue. Eventually they became known as just Nazz. They never really hit it big but did have a couple of minor hits with "Open My Eyes" and "Hello It's Me." The latter became a big hit for Rundgren after he pursued a solo career.

"Open My Eyes" was a song they expected might hit, but it didn't do much until a DJ accidentally played the flip side, "Hello It's Me." That song then became a hit and subsequently radio stations then started playing the flip side "Open My Eyes" as well, and it made a resurgence.

My favorite Nazz tunes
>'69: "Open My Eyes"
>'69: "Hello It's Me"

HOW THE HECK DID THEY GET THOSE NAMES? 149

NEW SEEKERS

Original members
> Eve Graham, lead vocals
> Lyn Paul
> Peter Doyle
> Marty Kristian
> Paul Martin Layton

This group started in London, England, in 1969. Keith Potger, who was an original member of the Australian group the Seekers put the band together but then retired from performing to become their producer. It was Potger who came up with the name the New Seekers (some original thinking there).

The New Seekers were mostly a pop group and did have a couple of hits both in the UK and the US. Their accomplishments included "I'd Like to Teach the World to Sing," "You Won't Find Another Fool Like Me," "Beg, Steal or Borrow," and "What Have They Done to My Song, Ma," which had a slightly different title in the US as "Look What They've Done to My Song, Ma."

My favorite New Seekers songs
> '70: "Look What They've Done to My Song, Ma"
> '71: "I'd Like to Teach the World to Sing"
> '73: "You Won't Find Another Fool Like Me" (that's one I sing
to my wife all the time)

150   RON TAVERNIT

NEW VAUDEVILLE BAND

Original members (their names are the reason I included this group in this endeavor)

Tristam, Seventh Earl of Cricklewood, vocals
"Moody" Mick Wilsher, vocals, guitar
Stan Haywod, a.k.a. Stanley K. Wood, piano
"Mad" Heri Harrison, drums, spoons, washboard, percussion
Robert "Pops" Kerr, trumpet
Neil Korner, bass (how'd he get in here)
Hugh "Shuggy" Watts, trombone

A record producer named Geoff Stephens wrote a song called "Winchester Cathedral" and put a group of studio musicians together in England to record it. It was a novelty song, so no one thought it would become a hit. Wow! Were they wrong. The song used a megaphone vocal like that of the twenties and hit number 1 in the US and was a top ten hit in the UK. It sold over three million copies and won a Grammy Award in 1967.

No one knows who all the original musicians were that recorded the song, but above are the members of the group that began to tour after the song's release. It was put together because there were so many requests since the song became a hit. Some of the members were from another group called the Bonzo Dog Doo-Dah Band (now that's a name I like).

My favorite New Vaudeville band song
'66: "Winchester Cathedral"

NITTY GRITTY DIRT BAND

Original members
Jeff Hanna, lead vocals, guitar, washboard, harmonica
Glen Grosclose, guitar
Ralph Barr, guitar, banjo
Les Thompson, guitar, banjo (how many banjos to you need)
Bruce Kunkel, guitar, banjo, fiddle (oops, I guess that answers that question)
David Hanna, bass, drums, percussion

This group started out of Long Beach, California, in 1966 with Hanna and Kunkel as the Long Beach Two, the New Coast Two, and the Illegitimate Jug Band (now that's an interesting name). According to some sources the duo was "trying to figure out how not to have to work for a living" (typical California style).

After adding four more members, they became known as the Jug Band. In 1967, they decided to call themselves the Nitty Gritty Dirt Band.

Interesting note: In 1977, they became to first group from the US to be invited to tour in the Soviet Union. They played several dozen concerts and appeared on Soviet TV watched by nearly 150 million people.

My favorite Nitty Gritty Dirt Band songs
'70: "Mr. Bojangles"
'72: "Jambalaya"
'74: "The Battle of New Orleans"

OHIO PLAYERS

Original members
- Leroy "Sugar" Bonner, lead guitar
- Bruce Napier, trumpet
- Marvin "Merve" Pierce, flugelhorn
- Andrew Noland, sax
- Clarence "Satch" Satchell, replaced Noland
- Walter Morrison, keyboards
- William "Billy" Beck, replaced Morrison
- Ralph Middlebrooks, trumpet
- Marshall "Rock" Jones, bass
- Robert Ward, vocals, guitar (band leader)
- Greg Webster, drums
- Clarence "Chet" Willis, rhythm guitar

This group started as Greg Webster and the Ohio Untouchables from Dayton, Ohio, in the early sixties. The group had a number of altercations with their leader, Robert Ward. Ward would sometimes walk off stage in the middle of a show. At one point, he and Jones got into a fight, and Ward was replaced by Leroy "Sugarfoot" Bonner.

In 1965, the group changed their name to the Ohio Players because all the members of the band considered themselves "ladies' men" (ahhh, I get it, Ohio *players!*).

My favorite Ohio Players song
- '74: "Skin Tight"

O'JAYS

Original members
    Walter Williams
    Edward Levert
    William Powell
    William Isles
    Robert Massey

This R & B quintet formed in Canton, Ohio, in 1958. All the members were from the same high school at the time and took the name the Mascots and later called themselves the Triumphs. After a few years of moderate success, they met Cleveland disc jockey Eddie O'Jay, who helped manage and produce the group from that point on. As a tribute to their newfound buddy, they changed their name to the O'Jays.

The O'Jays did have some success as an R & B touring group but never hit with the chart-buster they yearned for. That all changed in 1972. Two members of the group, Bill Isles and Robert Massey, left and the group became a trio. Then they hit big with the million-seller "Back Stabbers." That was followed by "Love Train" and a number of other hits.

The O'Jays were inducted into the Vocal Group Hall of Fame in 2004 followed by the Rock and Roll Hall of Fame in 2005 and the National Rhythm and Blues Hall of Fame in 2013.

My favorite O'Jays songs
    '72: "Back Stabbers"
    '73: "Love Train"

ORIGINALS

Original members
> Fred Gorman
> Henry Dixon
> Walter Gaines
> Crathman Spencer

This group has been heard on more Motown songs than most people realize. Some call them Motown's best kept secret. They were background singers for Jimmy Ruffin, Stevie Wonder, Edwin Starr, Marvin Gaye, and many more and were featured on several of their top recordings. However, in most cases, they were never given credit for what they did.

They also had some great commercial success. In 1969, they released their album *Baby, I'm for Real* with a single of the same title. It sold more than a million copies and received a Gold Disc from the Recording Industry Association of America.

There really is no information about how the Originals got their name, but I included them because they were so good and so few people knew about them.

My favorite Originals songs
> '69: "Baby, I'm for Real"
> '69: "The Bells"

ORLEANS

Original members
- John Hall, vocals, lead guitar
- Lance Hoppen, bass
- Lawrence Hoppen, lead vocals, guitar
- Wells Kelly, vocals, organ
- Jerry Marotta, drums

You might expect this group came from New Orleans, Louisiana, but that would be wrong. This group was started in 1972 by John Hall, who was a guitarist and composer in New York City. Hall had help from Larry Hoppen who sang and played guitar and keyboards, and Wells Kelly, who played drums. Later that year Larry's brother Lance, who played bass, joined the group.

The name Orleans came from the music the group performed specially from the style of the Neville Brothers. While Hall was from New York City. The group was organized in Woodstock, New York. Orleans had two major hits, "Dance with Me," which reached number 6 on the Billboard Hot 100 in 1975, and "Still the One" reached number 5 a year later. In 1977, the song was used as the theme for the ABC TV network and has been used in numerous commercials and even some movie soundtracks. (Wow! I'd love to see the royalty checks from those deals!)

Interesting note: John Hall was elected into the US House of Representatives in 2006.

My favorite Orleans songs
- '75: "Dance with Me"
- '76: "Still the One"

THE OUTSIDERS

Original members
    Sonny Geraci, lead vocals
    William Bruno, lead guitar
    Tom King, rhythm guitar
    Merdin Prince Gunner "Mert" Madsen, bass, harmonica (long
name)

This group started in 1965 with Tom King and "Mert" Madsen. Their original name was the Starfires and featured members from local clubs in and around the Cleveland, Ohio, area.

After recording their biggest hit, "Time Won't Let Me," they changed their name to the "Outsiders." The song was written by Tom King and his brother-in-law, Chet Kelley. One story suggests they made the change because after recording the song the group left their record company even though it was owned by King's uncle, Patrick Connelly, head of Pama Records. The group went on to Capitol Records with their new hit. The story goes on to say that King and Kelley were then regarded as outsiders because they left the family business. Another story says the name change was something that Capitol Records wanted.

"Time Won't Let Me" was a top 10 song in 1966 and sold over a million records.

My favorite Outsiders song
    '66: "Time Won't Let Me"

OZARK MOUNTAIN DAREDEVILS

Original members
    Randle Chowning, lead guitar
    John Dillon, guitar, fiddle, mandolin
    Buddy Brayfield, keyboards
    Steven Cash, harmonica, percussion
    Michael "Supe" Granda, bass
    Lawrence Lee, drums

I love this group because of the variety of names they had. This group started in Springfield, Missouri, as the Family Tree, the Emergency Band, Buffalo Chips & Burlap Socks (that's my favorite), Rhythm of Joy, and Cosmic Corncob & His Amazing Mountain Daredevils (another fave)!

Apparently, Michael "Supe" Granda (that's Granda, not Grandpa, just to be clear) wrote a book and says the group came up with their name from their last name before, which was Cosmic Corn Cob & His Amazing Mountain Daredevils. He says guitarist John Dillon came up with the idea because one of their other names (Family Tree) was already being used by another group. He also suggested that all the other members of the band did not want to be referred to as Cosmic Corn Cob (Why! I think it's great!). Anyway, at that point, they shortened the name to Ozark Mountain Daredevils.

Favorite Ozark Mountain Daredevils songs
    '74: "If You Want to get to Heaven"
    '75: "Jackie Blue"

PROCOL HARUM

Original members
> Ray Royer, lead guitar
> Gary Brooker, keyboards
> Matthew Fisher, keyboards
> David Knights, bass
> Robert Harrison, drums
> Keith Reid, lyricist

This English Rock band started in 1967. They were originally known as the Paramounts and after moderate success renamed themselves the Pinewoods. After some personnel changes, their manager, Guy Stevens, came up with the name Procol Harum. That was the name of a cat owned by a woman Stevens knew. The cat's actual name however was Procul Harun.

The group's major claim to fame was the recording of "A Whiter Shade of Pale," which had a hint of the 1600 and 1700s baroque and classical styles. It was also one of the rare singles that sold over ten million copies.

My favorite Procol Harum song
> '67: "A Whiter Shade of Pale"

Paper Lace

Original members
    Philip Wright, vocals, drums
    Michael Vaughn, guitar
    Chris Morris, guitar
    Carlo Santanna (not Carlos Santana), rhythm guitar
    Cliff Fish (not cat fish, ha ha), bass

This group started as the Music Box in 1967 out of Nottingham, England. In 1969, they changed their name to Paper Lace due to the fact that Nottingham was called the Lace City.

The group really did not have much success until 1973. In that year, they won several local television show performance contests and were signed to a record label called Bus Stop. In 1974, under their new label, they recorded their first hit "Billy, Don't Be a Hero," about the American Civil War. The song was a big hit in the UK but didn't do much for Paper Lace. However, Bo Donaldson and the Heywoods recorded a cover of the song, which became an enormous hit for them. Soon after, Paper Lace recorded another hit called "The Night Chicago Died," which reached number 1 here in the US.

My favorite Paper Lace songs
    '74: "Billy, Don't Be a Hero"
    '74: "Night Chicago Died"

PAUL MCCARTNEY AND WINGS

Original members
Paul McCartney, lead vocals, bass
Denny Laine, guitar
Linda McCartney, keyboards
Henry McCollough, guitar
Denny Seiwell, drums

After Paul had recorded a couple of solo albums with the help of a number of musician friends, he decided to form a new group. He asked Denny Seiwell to join him and his wife, Linda, to put the group together. He also asked Denny Laine to join, and he accepted even though he was working on his own album at the time.

The name of the band came as a result of Paul's wife, Linda, giving birth to their daughter, Stella. Paul says there were complications and that both his wife and new baby daughter almost died. While praying for Linda and Stella, his mind kept featuring the image of wings. That became the new name of his band!

Interesting note: Paul was arrested upon arriving in Japan in January 1980 due to possession of over seven ounces of marijuana. He spent ten days in jail before being released and deported. Obviously, his tour in Japan was cancelled even though over one hundred thousand tickets had been sold. The group disbanded in 1981. Over the years, they had fourteen top 10 hits in the US and ten in the UK.

My favorite Paul McCartney and Wings songs
'71: "Uncle Albert / Admiral Halsey"
'72: "Give Ireland Back to the Irish"
'73: "Live and Let Die"
'74: "Band on the Run"
'75: "Listen to What the Mad Said"
'76: "Silly Little Love Songs"

QUEEN

Original members
  Freddie "Mercury" Bulsara, lead vocals, keyboards
  Brian May, guitar
  John Deacon, bass
  Roger Meadows Taylor, drums

This group formed out of London, England, in 1970. Queen featured Freddie Bulsara (Mercury), Brian May, Roger Taylor, and John Deacon. In the late sixties, Bulsara is said to have been a fan of the group Smile, which featured May and Taylor. The group's lead singer was Tim Staffell and Bulsara asked to join the group as their singer. Other members of Smile thought Staffell would have a problem with that, but he soon left the group anyway to form Humpy Bong. At this point, Smile then accepted Bulsara, who was from Zanzabar, India, as their lead singer.

Bulsara suggested a new name for the group, Queen. The other members weren't hot on the idea, but Bulsara persisted, saying, "It's wonderful, people will love it." At that point, they became known as Queen and Bulsara then changed his name to Mercury. The word *mercury* comes from the lyrics of the song "Fairy King."

My favorite Queen songs
  '76: "Bohemian Rhapsody"
  '77: "We Are the Champions" (I keep hoping we can use that song when the Detroit Lions win a championship! Hey, they came close!)

QUESTION MARK AND THE MYSTERIANS

Original members
  Larry Borjas, guitar
  Robert Martinez, drums
  Bobby Balderrama, lead guitar
  Rudy Martinez (Question Mark), lead vocals

This group got together in 1962 in the Bay City/Saginaw area of Michigan even though all the original members were from Mexico. Rudy Martinez, his brother Robert, and Larry Borjas were the original members. Robert and Larry apparently joined the Army (to avoid being sent to Vietnam) prior to the groups big hit. At that point, Question Mark and the Mysterians added other members and then had their one huge hit, "96 Tears." That song, from 1966, was a number 1 national hit and was the most requested song at Flint's WTAC and the Detroit area (Windsor, Ontario, Canada) station CKLW.

The name Question Mark and the Mysterians actually has a bit of mystery to it. Question Mark is actually Rudy Martinez, even though he will never admit or confirm it. In an interview, I did with him (somewhere around 2005), he claims to have come from Mars (What? Threw me for a loop too) and that Question Mark is his actual name. In reality, Rudy had his name legally changed to Question Mark. However, he wanted it to be the symbol? rather than the words. The court wouldn't accept that and insisted the name Question Mark would have to be spelled out. Rudy accepted (didn't have a choice, I guess), and that part is now history.

As to the Mysterians, the group says it was inspired by the movie *The Mysterians* from the late fifties. The group disbanded in 1968 and in 1981 made a comeback with new members.

Back to Question Mark. He became a dog breeder and moved to Clio, Michigan (near the center of the state). In 2007, a fire destroyed his home and killed most of his dogs. Following that trag-edy, a number of his friends and fans helped him by promoting a number of benefit shows. Question Mark and the Mysterians (new group) performed.

My favorite Question Mark and the Mysterians songs
'66: "96 Tears"
'66: "I Need Somebody"

REFLECTIONS

Original members
> Tony Micale, lead vocals
> Phil Castrodale, first tenor
> Daniel Bennie, second tenor
> Ray Steinberg, baritone
> John Dean, bass

I must admit the Reflections hold a special place in my heart for a number of reasons. Current members are good friends of mine, and I have had the good fortune of being MC of a number of their concerts over the years.

The name Reflections was used by a number of groups over the years. Among them was the group Chad Allen and the Reflections, later to be known as the Guess Who. However, when they heard that this group had a big hit song ("Romeo and Juliet"), they changed their name back to Chad Allen and the Expressions. Now there is also a great story on how Chad Allen and the Expressions wound up as the Guess Who (please see "Guess Who").

The Reflections started in the early '60s in Detroit as a blue-eyed soul–doo-opp group. As a matter of fact, they are still known as the Deacons of Doo-Oop (I believe it was Honey Radio DJ Fred Boogie Brian that coined the term). Their song "(Just Like) Romeo & Juliet" was a top 10 hit on a number of National Charts. They followed that up with "Like Columbus Did" and, one of my all-time favorites, "Shabby Little Hut"—all from 1964.

Here's an interesting tidbit: As a member of the on-air staff at Honey Radio (WHND) in Detroit, we were told the Reflections were recording personalized jingles for the staff. One evening, I received a call from Gary Banovitz (a newer member of the group), who told me they couldn't find anything to rhyme with my last name, Tavernit. They wanted to record the jingle as Ron T. I said yes, go ahead, and that became my on-air name for the next twenty years or more. I could go on and on with so many good memories.

The timing of the emergence of the Reflections was a bit unfortunate because it coincided with groups like the Beatles, the rest of the British Invasion, Motown, and the California surf sound. Imagine having to compete with those groups. However, they did get some recognition as their picture is featured in the Rock and Roll Hall of Fame in Cleveland.

My favorite Reflections songs
    '64: "(Just Like) Romeo & Juliet"
    '64: "Like Columbus Did"
    '64: "Shabby Little Hut"
    '65: "Poor Man's Son"

REO SPEEDWAGON

Original members
  Terry Luttrell, vocals
  Greg Philbin, bass
  Gary Richrath, guitar
  Neal Doughty, keyboards
  Alan Gratzer, drums

This group formed at the University of Illinois in 1968. At first, they performed as an opening act for several other higher profile bands, like Bob Seger and Kansas. Starting in the 1970s, they achieved great success. Their best-selling LP called *Hi Infidelity* (love the title) has sold over ten-million copies.

The band came up with their unusual name when Neal Doughty saw the name on a blackboard in his history of transportation class. It was the name of a truck originating from 1915 and designed by Lansing, Michigan, native Ransom Eli Olds. Hence, the car company name Oldsmobile. Originally the company called the vehicle REE-O (two syllables) Speedwagon as opposed to R-E-O Speedwagon. The group took the later.

My favorite REO Speedwagon songs
  '80: "Keep on Lovin You"
  '80: "Take it on the Run"
  '82: "Keep the Fire Burnin'"

RICHARD HELL AND THE VOIDOIDS

Richard "Hell" Meyers
Robert Quine
Ivan Julian
Marc Bell
Marky Ramone

You're probably wondering who the hell (excuse the play on words) is Richard Hell and the Voidoids. Actually, I'm wondering the same thing. Richard Hell was actually Richard Meyers, who dropped out of high school in Kentucky then moved to New York City. He and a guy named Tom Miller became the Neon Boys rock band in the early seventies. The Neon Boys eventually became the group Television and eventually broke up. Richard renamed himself as Richard Hell because he said that's how he felt (like hell, I guess).

At this point, Richard worked with a number of groups for a short amount of time until he found other members inclined to be like him and perform like him, which was punk rock. The other members decided to call themselves the Voidoids taken from a book Hell was in the process of writing.

One other note is that Richard liked to perform in torn clothing held together with safety pins.

Some of my favorite Richard Hell and the Voidoids songs
"Zip-a-d-du-da" (punk rock was never my thing)—I just had to include them in this for no other reason than their ridiculous name

Rick Dees and His Cast of Idiots

Rigdon Osmond Dees III is probably best known for being a radio personality and for "The Rick Dees Weekly Top 40 Countdown." After over twenty years on KIIS radio in Los Angeles, he left the show and was replaced by, none other than, Ryan Seacrest.

Dees did have some success as a recording artist having written and recorded a huge national hit called "Disco Duck." Dees did not perform the duck voice on the song, which job went to a guy named Ken Pruitt and later to Michael Chesney. One wonders if those must have been his Cast of Idiots.

My favorite Rick Dees and His Cast of Idiots song
  '76: "Disco Duck"

RIGHTEOUS BROTHERS

Original members
 Bill Medley
 Bobby Hatfield

The Righteous Brothers began in a group called the Paramours in 1962 out of Los Angeles, California. Sometime later, they decided to form a duo. Bill Medley had a beautiful bass voice and Hatfield was a powerful tenor. Obviously, they were not brothers. They came up with the name when a black fan referred to them as righteous. That was a term popular in the black community in the early sixties. Since they were a duo, they took the name and called themselves brothers. And the Righteous Brothers were born.

In 1963, they had a minor hit with "Little Latin Lupe Lu" and, one year later, hit with "You've Lost That Lovin' Feelin'," when it hit number 1 on the pop charts and number 3 on R & B. Several other hits followed.

Over the years, Hatfield and Medley would separate and follow solo careers but got back together at various times. Unfortunately, Bobby Hatfield died in 2003 in a Kalamazoo, Michigan, hotel prior to a scheduled performance with Medley.

The Righteous Brothers were inducted into the Rock and Roll Hall of Fame in 2003 and were members of the Greatest Duos of All Time. They also had a number of other awards and accolades.

My favorite Righteous Brothers songs
 '63: "Little Latin Lupe Lu"
 '64: "You've Lost That Lovin' Feelin'"
 '66: "Ebb Tide"
 '66: "You're My Soul and Inspiration"
 '74: "Rock and Roll Heaven"

THE ROLLING STONES

Original members
Michael Philip, Jagger, lead vocals
Keith Richard, lead guitar
Brian Jones, rhythm guitar
Ian Stewart, keyboard
Charlie Watts, drums

The Rolling Stones are considered one of, if not, the greatest rock group of all time. The Stones got together in 1962 in London. Prior to that, Jagger put together a garage band with his early boyhood friend, Dick Taylor. At that time, they played a lot of R &B tunes from the US, including music from Chuck Berry, Little Richard, Muddy Waters, and others. Jagger and Keith Richards knew each other from Dartford Maypole County Primary School in the early fifties and became reacquainted in 1960. Richards then decided to join Jagger and became a member of this new group in 1961 and called themselves the Blues Boys.

In 1962, the Blues Boys sent a tape of their music to Alexis Korner, who was head of the Alexis Korner's Rhythm and Blues Band. Korner was impressed with the group and had them meet his other members, including Brian Jones, Ian Stewart, and Charlie Watts. At that point, Jagger and Richards started playing with the group and renamed their band Alexis Kroner's Blues Incorporated. Jones and Stewart left the group, and soon after Jagger and Richards left as well to join them.

According to Keith Richards, Jones is responsible for naming the band. Jones was on the phone with a guy from a local jazz magazine, who asked him what the name of his group was. According to Richards, he looked on the floor and saw one of Muddy Waters LPs with a song called "Rollin' Stone," and as they say, the rest is history.

Over the years, the Stones were involved in a number of infamous events, including several drug arrests and a killing involving the Hells Angels motorcycle gang while they performed at a raceway in California.

The Stones were inducted into the Rock and Roll Hall of Fame in 1989. Other awards and accolades are just too numerous to mention, but many believe they were, and still are, the greatest rock and roll band in music history.

The Stones legacy even reached a group of scientists who named seven fossil stoneflies after members of the band, including the *Petroperia michjaggeri* and *Lasiperia keithrichardsi* and others in honor of the Rolling Stones and referred to the fossils as Rolling stoneflies. In the US, NASA named a rock on the planet Mars Rolling Stone Rock because the Mars Lander *InSight* nudged a rock when it landed there, and it must have rolled a bit.

My favorite Rolling Stones songs
'64: "Not Fade Away"
'64: "It's All over Now"
'64: "Time Is on My Side"
'65: "Satisfaction" (the number 1 song of the entire year)
'65: "The Last Time"
'65: "Get Off My Cloud"
'66: "19th Nervous Breakdown"
'66: "Paint It Black"
'66: "Mother's Little Helper"
'67: "Ruby Tuesday"
'67: "Let's Spend the Night Together"
'68: "Jumpin' Jack Flash"
'69: "Honkey-Tonk Women"
'71: "Brown Sugar"
'73: "You Can't Always Get What You Want"
'74: "Ain't Too Proud to Beg"

SAM THE SHAM & THE PHARAOHS

Original members
   Sam the Sham (Domingo Samudio), lead vocals, keyboards
   Ray Stinnet, lead guitar
   David Martin, bass
   Jerry Patterson, drums
   Butch Gibson, sax

Domingo Samudio got his start as early as second grade singing in school. In high school, he started playing guitar and joined a group that also featured Trini Lopez. Following graduation, he joined the Navy and acquired the name Big Sam.

In 1963, Sam joined a group called the Nightriders. The group performed at a night club in Louisiana until June of that year. At that point, the Nightriders moved to Memphis, Tennessee.

After a couple of personnel changes in Memphis, the group decided to change their name. Sam called himself Sam the Sham because other members joked about his inability to sing. Note: Some said the Sham part of the name came from the way Sam danced on stage (shamming—got to admit, I'm not much of a dancer, but what the hell is shamming?). Then they decided on the name Pharaohs for the band that was inspired by the costumes worn in the movie *The Ten Commandments*. (They must have been fans of Yul Brynner. I wonder if they shaved their heads?) Sam the Sham and the Pharaohs was born.

To support their new name, the group wore turbans and robes during their performances. The group became very popular in the midsixties with big hits like "Wooly Bully" and "Lil Red Riding Hood," both hitting number 2 on the rock and roll charts.

My favorite Sam the Sham and the Pharaohs songs
'65: "Wooly Bully"
'65: "Lil Red Riding Hood"
'66: "The Hair on My Chinny Chin Chin"

THE SANDPIPERS

Original members
  James Brady
  Richard Shoff
  Michael Piano (there's a good name for a musician)

This trio started in the early sixties as members of the Mitchell Boys Choir out of Los Angeles, California. After leaving the choir, they formed a quartet by adding their friend, Nick Cahuernga, to the group. At this point, they called themselves the Four Seasons. However, there was another group that was in the process of becoming popular at the time with the same name, so they changed their name to the Grads. They lost Cahuernga from the group, so they became a trio once again.

After recording several songs that did not fare well in the marketplace, they came to the attention of Herb Alpert, who was impressed and signed them to a record contract. It was at that time they felt they needed a new name and took the moniker Sandpipers from the birds of the same name that frequented the beaches of California. In 1966, they recorded "Guantanamera," which became a top 10 hit. Later in 1969, they scored their biggest hit with the theme song for the movie *The Sterile Cuckoo* called "Come Saturday Morning."

"Guantanamera" earned Grammy nominations in 1967 for Best Performance by a Vocal Group and Best Contemporary Group Performance.

My favorite Sandpipers songs
  '66: "Guantanamera"
  '69: "Come Saturday Morning"

SCREAMIN' JAY HAWKINS

Jalacy Hawkins was born in 1929 in Cleveland, Ohio, and was raised by foster parents. Hawkins took piano lessons and performed in neighborhood bars for tip money. Later, he won a Golden Gloves boxing championship at fourteen years old and in 1949 won the middleweight championship in Alaska.

In 1953, Hawkins teamed up with Tiny Grimes's band and became known for his outlandish style. In 1955, he went solo and adopted the Screamin' moniker due to his flamboyant rock style. He would wear leopard-skin clothes, red jackets, and wild hats. Hawkins would carry a skull on a stick and other voodoo paraphernalia while performing as well. Infamous disc jockey Alan Freed even convinced Hawkins to enter the stage from a coffin.

Screamin' Hawkins's most successful recording was "I Put a Spell on You" in 1956. That song was said to be one of the Rock and Roll Hall of Fame's 500 Songs That Shaped Rock and Roll. Hawkins also recorded a song called "Constipation Blues" because no one else had ever done a song about "real pain." The song contained a lot of grunts and groans and was even performed with Hawkins on stage sitting on a toilet (try to get that image out of your head, you're welcome)!

My favorite Screamin' Jay Hawkins songs
'56: "I Put a Spell on You"
'70: "Constipation Blues"

THE SEARCHERS

Original members
>   Anthony Jackson, lead vocals
>   Michael Pendergast, lead guitar
>   John McNally, rhythm guitar
>   Chris Curtis, drums

This group formed in 1960 out of Liverpool, England. They were known as clean-cut performers with great harmonies. They were originally the backup group for singer Johnny Sandon.

The Searchers established themselves by becoming regulars, playing at the Iron Door club in Liverpool. They were considered part of the Mersey beat genre along with the Beatles, the Hollies, Gerry and the Pacemakers, and others of the British Invasion. Like a number of other groups, America got its taste of the Searchers when they appeared on *The Ed Sullivan Show*.

The Searchers acquired their name from the *John Ford* movie of the same title.

My favorite Searchers songs
>   '64: "Needles and Pins"
>   '64: "Sugar and Spice"
>   '64: "Don't Throw Your Love Away"
>   '64: "Love Potion #9"

SHA NA NA

Original members
    Fredrick "Dennis" Greene
    "Screamin" Scott Simon
    John "Jocko" Marcellino
    Donald York
    John "Bowser" Bauman
    Tony Santini
    Lenn Baker
    Johnny Contardo
    Dave "Chico" Ryan
    Dan McBride

These guys started in 1969 at Columbia University as an a cappella singing group. They originally performed at a fifties dance at Columbia. Their talent caught on, and they decided to go professional.

The group was originally known as the Kingsmen, but another group already used it and had a big hit song called "Louie Louie." So they changed their name and came up with "Sha Na Na," which came from the song "Get a Job" by the Silhouettes. (In that song, the words "sha na na na, sha na na na na" were a major part of the lyrics.)

"Sha Na Na" got a huge break after getting an invitation to perform at the Woodstock Festival in 1969. They were known as rock and roll / doo-wop singers reviving the music of the fifties and sixties as well as a unique comedy style. They were best known, however, for their hit TV series that ran from 1977 to 1981, also called *Sha Na Na*. The group really never had a hit song, but their TV show took off and had great ratings. They also appeared in the hit movie *Grease*.

During their TV series, they would perform such comedic tunes like "Hello Muddah, Hello Faddah" and "Alley Oop."

SHADOWS OF KNIGHT

Original members
    Sim Sohns, lead vocals, percussion
    Joseph Kelley, lead guitar, bass, harp
    Warren Rogers, guitar, bass
    Jerry McGeorge, rhythm guitar
    Thomas Schiffour, drums

This group started in the garages of the Chicago suburbs and concentrated on British tunes in the midsixties. They described their style as taking the music of a number of British Invasion groups and giving their songs an English interpretation.

When they began, they initially called themselves the Shadows but found out there was already a London group of the same name. At that point, a record shop owner, Whiz Winters, who knew the group's manager, Paul Sampson, suggested the Shadows of Knight. Whiz (sorry, but I gotta use that name again, what was his mother thinking anyway) said all the band members were from the same high school, Prospect, from Mt. Prospect, Illinois, and their team mascot was the Knights. Everyone approved, and the Shadows of Knight was born.

In 1965, the group released a remake of Van Morrison's song "Gloria." They replaced the Morrison lyrics of "she comes to my room, then she made me feel all right" with "she called out my name, that made me feel all right." The reason for the change was the original was banned on Chicago radio stations due to the implications of the Morrison song (wow, look at the lyrics you can get away with now). "Gloria" became a big hit, ranking tenth on the Billboard charts and number 1 on a number of Chicago stations. The record sold over a million copies.

My favorite Shadows of Knight songs
    '66: "Gloria"
    '66: "I'm Gonna Make You Mine"

SHANGRI-LAS

Original members
>Mary Weiss, lead vocals
>Betty Weiss, vocals
>Mary Anne Ganser, vocals
>Marge Ganser, vocals

The Shangri-Las consisted of four women, two sets of sisters. The Ganser sisters were actually identical twins. They were all high school classmates from Andrew Jackson High in Queens, New York.

The girls were good singers and played a number of local talent shows and hops before signing a record deal with Kama Sutra Records. (Now there's a name for a bunch of beautiful young women. Where were their dads?). In 1964, the girls signed a new deal with Red Bird Records (dads probably looked up *kama sutra* in the dictionary).

At first, the four girls performed without a formal name but decided on Shangri-Las after one of their favorite restaurants in Queens. After recording their first major hit, "Remember (Walkin' in the Sand)" in 1964, they followed up with their biggest hit, "The Leader of the Pack," which soared to number 1. The Shangri-Las had several more hits after that.

Unfortunately one of the twins, Mary Ganser, died of a drug overdose in 1970. The group continued for a while as a trio.

My favorite Shangri-Las songs
>'64: "Remember (Walkin' in the Sand)"
>'64: "Leader of the Pack"
>'64: "Give Him a Great Big Kiss"

SHIRELLES

Original members
    Shirley Owens
    Doris Coley
    Addie "Micki" Harris
    Beverly Lee

These four girls got together in 1957 in Passaic, New Jersey. They performed under the name Poquellos. They entered a talent show at their high school and were heard by a classmate whose mother was in the music business. The mom, Florence Greenberg, was the owner of Tiara Records.

At first, the girls weren't interested in singing professionally but finally agreed to a booking. At that point, they decided to change their name and came up with the Shirelles. The name came from the first syllable in Shirley Owens name and another popular group at the time, the Chantels.

The Shirelles were best known for their rhythm and blues / doo-wop sound as well as soul. The girls were also known for writing their own songs, which was a rarity for the time. The Shirelles had the look of young school girls, but much of their music had sexual overtones. Their music was also said to be a reflection of the civil rights movement.

This group was inducted into the Rock and Roll Hall of Fame in 1996 and was named one of the 100 Greatest Artists of All Time by *Rolling Stone* magazine in 2004.

My favorite Shirelles songs
    '60: "Tonight's the Night"
    '60: "Will You Love Me Tomorrow"
    '61: "Dedicated to the One I Love"
    '61: "Mama Said"
    '61: "Baby It's You"
    '61: "Soldier Boy"
    '63: "Foolish Little Girl"

SIMON AND GARFUNKEL

Paul Simon and Art Garfunkel were schoolmates from the age of twelve in Queens, New York. Soon after meeting, they began to sing and harmonize together. In 1957, they sang one of Paul's originals, "Hey Schoolgirl." An agent heard them and signed them up with Big Records. At that time, they called themselves Tom and Jerry. Some have speculated the name came from the cartoon characters. They also made an appearance on American Bandstand. Soon after, Tom and Jerry split up. Sources say there was always a degree of animosity between the two.

In 1963, they got back together, this time as Simon and Garfunkel, and signed with Columbia Records. Their first effort, an album called *Wednesday Morning, 3am*, did not do well, and Simon and Garfunkel split up again. In 1965, Simon was performing in London and found out one of his songs from *Wednesday Morning, 3am* became number 1 in the US. The song "Sounds of Silence" was then remixed to a more folksy style. Simon and Garfunkel were now back together and performing on the college circuit.

In 1967, they got a huge break when their music was featured in the movie *The Graduate*. From that point, their songs "The Sounds of Silence," "Mrs. Robinson," "The Boxer," and "Bridge over Troubled Water" all reached number 1.

In 1970, the duo broke up again, and both resumed solo careers. Simon and Garfunkel won ten Grammys over their careers and were elected into the Rock and Roll Hall of Fame in 1990.

My Favorite Simon and Garfunkel songs
'65: "Sounds of Silence"
'66: "I Am a Rock"
'68: "Scarborough Fair"
'68: "Mrs. Robinson"
'70: "Bridge over Troubled Water"
'70: "Cecelia"
'72: "Mother and Child Reunion" (Simon solo)

'72: "Me and Julio Down by the Schoolyard" (Simon)
'73: "Kodachrome" (Simon)
'77: "Slip Slidin' Away" (Simon)

SIR DOUGLAS QUINTET

Original members
  Douglas Saldana Sahm (Sir Douglas), lead vocals, guitar
  Augie Meyer, keyboards
  Jack Barber, bass
  Leon Beatty, percussion
  John Perez, drums

Doug Sahm started performing as a six-year-old on a San Antonio, Texas, radio station KMAC. At fifteen, he formed the Markays and then the Spirits and actually recorded with them.

After Houston producer Huey Meaux heard them, he signed them to a recording contract with his Tribe label. At this point, Douglas decided to change the name of his group and called himself Sir Douglas to give the impression the group was British and part of the British Invasion (an interesting idea, considering they were all from Texas).

The Sir Douglas Quintet had one major hit, "She's about a Mover" in 1966.

My favorite Sir Douglas Quintet song
  ' 66: "She's about a Mover" (you got it!)

SLY AND THE FAMILY STONE

Original members
  Sylvester Stewart, lead vocals, keyboards
  Fred Stewart, guitar
  Cynthia Robinson, trumpet
  Jerry Martini, sax
  Rose Stewart, keyboards

This group got together in the San Francisco area in 1966. It was that year that Sly Stewart became Sly Stone, which is what he called himself, and formed the group Sly and the Stoners (probably a reference to getting stoned on pot, which was certainly very popular at that time). At about that same time, Sly's brother, Freddie, also had a band called Freddie & the Stone Souls. The two groups decided to combine and became known as Sly Brothers and Sisters (the group also featured Sly's and Freddie's sister, Rose). After one gig, they decided to change the name again, and Sly and the Family Stone emerged. The group became well-known for their psychedelic soul genre. Interesting note: Sly Stone was also known as a popular DJ on KDIA Radio in San Francisco (never trust one of those DJ guys!).

Their first big hit was "Dance to the Music" in 1968 and reached the top 10 on Billboard's Hot 100. Later that same year, they recorded their biggest hit "Everyday People," which hit number 1.

Sly and the Family Stone was invited to perform at Woodstock in 1969 and given rave revues. Soon after, they released "Hot Fun in the Summertime," which reached number 2 on Billboard.

My favorite Sly and the Family Stone songs
  '68: "Dance to the Music"
  '68: "Everyday People"
  '69: "I Want to Take You Higher"
  '69: "Hot Fun in the Summertime"

SMALL FACES

Original members
    Steven Marriot, lead vocals and guitar
    James Winston, keyboards
    Ronald Lane, bass
    Kenneth Jones, drums

Steve Marriot organized this group in the midsixties in London, England. He was a member of local groups like the Moments and the Frantics. He was also known as a child actor.

It was Marriot that came up with the band's unusual name. He suggested the word *small* because of the small height of all the members, and *faces* because it was a term used for someone important (okay, someone will have to explain that one to me!). Anyway, that's when Small Faces was born.

Interestingly, in 1968, Marriot decided to leave the group and join Humble Pie. That could have been a serious blow to the group, but they were able to replace him with Ron Wood and Rod Stewart (yes, that Rod Stewart). They both came from the Jeff Beck group. And they became even more successful. They also changed their name again and decided to use just the name Faces. (I guess they might have grown a bit.)

My favorite Small Faces songs
    '67: "Itchycoo Park"
    '68: "Tin Soldier"

SMOKEY ROBINSON AND THE MIRACLES

Original members
  Smokey Robinson
  Warren "Pete" Moore
  Ronnie White
  Clarence Dawson
  James Grice

The entire group went to school together at Northern High in Detroit. They actually started singing together, before high school, at eleven years old, when they were known as the Five Chimes. At some point in the midfifties, both Dawson and Grice left the group and were replaced by Emerson "Sonny" Rogers and Bobby Rogers (his cousin). Then in 1957, Sonny left the group, and his sister, Claudette Rogers, joined up. At this time, they were known as the Matadors.

In 1957, they met Berry Gordy Jr., who was impressed and recorded their song "Got a Job" as an answer to "Get a Job" by the Silhouettes. Before the song was released, though, the group changed their name from the Matadors to the Miracles, taking half of the name from the Miracletones. The song that was featured on End Records became a major crossroad for Gordy. "Got a Job" was reasonably successful, but Gordy only made (literally) a couple dollars. At that point, Smokey suggested that Gordy should start his own label. He did, and Tamla Records was born. Tamla became a subsidiary to Motown Records and the Motown Corporation. At that point, Motown records distributed only locally, and Chess Records handled the national distribution. The song hit the top 100 (number 93) on the pop charts and convinced Gordy to take Motown to the national level. Also, in 1959, Smokey and Claudette became an item and got married that year.

All through the sixties, Smokey wrote songs for the Miracles and several other Motown groups, like the Marvelettes, Mary Wells,

Marvin Gaye, and the Temptations. Bob Dylan described Smokey as "the greatest living poet in America."

Smokey and the Miracles had dozens of great hits, including Motown's first million seller and number 1 single "Shop Around" in 1960.

The group also had numerous awards, including becoming members of the Rock and Roll Hall of Fame. However, there were some serious issues involved with that award. In 1987, Smokey was inducted, but as a solo artist without the Miracles. The editor of *Goldmine* magazine said, "How did Smokey Robinson get inducted without the Miracles?" Pete Moore, who was the Miracles' bass singer, told the Cleveland *Plain Dealer*, "It was a slap in the face, very disappointing. We are the premier group of Motown. We were there before there was a Motown. We set the pace for all the other artists to come after us. We were a little older, and the other artists looked up to us. How could we not be in there?" In 2012, the Miracles were inducted into the hall, and the president and CEO of the Hall of Fame apologized and said it should have been done years earlier.

In 1967, the Miracles became known as Smokey Robinson and the Miracles.

My favorite Smokey Robinson and the Miracles songs
'60: "Shop Around"
'63: "Mickey's Monkey"
'63: "Going to a Go-Go"
'63: "You've Really Got a Hold on Me"
'65: "Ooo, Baby Baby"
'65: "Tracks of My Tears"
'67: "More Love"
'67: "I Second That Emotion"
'70: "Tears of a Clown"

SONNY & CHER

Original members
    Salvatore Philip Bono
    Cherilyn Sakisian LaPierre

Sonny and Cher were a husband-wife duo that became immensely popular throughout the sixties and seventies. Sonny was born in Detroit, Michigan, while Cher was born in El Centro, California. Why do I mention that, you might ask? Because Sonny and I both lived on the same street in the Motor City, Camden, on Detroit's east side. It was a long street, and Sonny was much older, so I never met him, but I still wanted to mention it. (I mean, how much talent can reside on one little side street? Okay, you can stop rolling your eyes.)

After moving to the West Coast, Sonny spent time writing music and singing under the name Don Christy. In 1964, Sonny cowrote the song "Needles and Pins," which became a big hit for the Searchers. Sonny became a primary writer for Phil Spector as well as a backup singer. After meeting Cher, both of them became backup singers for Spector's groups.

Sonny and Cher got married in 1964 and began singing under the name Caesar and Cleo. By 1965 they changed their names to Sonny and Cher and the hits started coming in! One of their first songs as Sonny and Cher was "I Got You Babe" that hit number 1.

By 1970, the duo became media personalities and had two highly rated TV Shows, *The Sonny & Cher Comedy Hour* and *The Sonny & Cher Show*. The couple divorced in 1975. Cher went on to a great solo career, and Sonny got into politics and was elected to the US House of Representatives. In 1998, Sonny was killed in a skiing accident. Later that same year, the duo received a star on the Hollywood Walk of Fame.

My favorite Sonny & Cher songs
    '65: "I Got You Babe"
    '65: "Baby Don't Go"

'66: "What Now My Love"
'67: "The Beat Goes On"
'71: "All I Ever Need Is You"

STANDELLS

Original members
> Lawrence Tamblyn, lead guitar
> Dick Dodd, rhythm guitar
> Gary Lane, bass
> Tony Valentino, drums

This group got together in 1962 and became one of the first punk groups in US history. Their major claim to fame is their recording of "Dirty Water" in 1966. That song is listed as one of the 500 Songs that Shaped Rock and Roll by the Rock and Roll Hall of Fame.

The group got their name after figuring they did a lot of standing around an agent's office waiting to be picked for work. Yep! That's how the Standells were born.

It is said their song "Dirty Water" is played after the Boston Red Sox and Boston Bruins win a home game. (Hey, what about the Celtics! Go figure!)

My favorite Standells song
> '66: "Dirty Water"

STATLER BROTHERS

Original members
    Lew C. DeWitt
    Don S. Reid
    Harold W. Reid
    Phillip E. Balsley

All four of these guys were friends in elementary school in Virginia where they started singing, but only two of them were actually brothers, and their last name was never Statler. The group performed gospel music in many of the local churches and country and gospel at other venues.

They started as a quartet in 1955 and called themselves the Four Star Quartet and later the Kingsmen. However, another group called the Kingsmen had a big hit song in 1963 called "Louie Louie," so they had to come up with something different. One day while in a hotel, where they were waiting to perform, they noticed a box of Statler tissues on the counter. And as they say, the rest is history. They said they could have named themselves the Kleenex Brothers (or maybe the Wipers or Blowers or Nosies).

The Statler Brothers auditioned for and were hired by Johnny Cash to be the opening act for many of his concerts over the years. However, they had one huge hit themselves in 1965 called "Flowers on the Wall." The group also did a song tribute to Johnny Cash called "We Got Paid by Cash" (Okay, I guess that makes sense.) The group was also featured on *The Johnny Cash Show* a number of times and had their own show on the Nashville Network called *The Statler Brothers Show*, where they were known not only for their country music efforts but for their comedy as well.

The Statler Brothers were very big on the country music scene. The group released forty albums over the years and achieved number 1 on the country charts four times. They were the Country Music Associations Vocal Group of the Year six times in a row and nine times total and inducted into the Country Music Hall of Fame and Museum in 2008 and the Gospel Hall of Fame in 2007.

My favorite Statler Brothers song
 '65: "Flowers on the Wall"

STEAM

Original members
> Gary DeCarlo, studio musician
> Dale Frashuer, studio musician
> Paul Leka, studio musician
> Garrett Scott, vocals
> Tom Zuke, vocals
> Hank Schorz, vocals
> Bill Steer, vocals

Interesting right off the bat! There really was no group called Steam. It all started with a group called the Chateaus featuring Paul Leka and Gary DeCarlo. The group was working on several songs and impressed Mercury Records.

The label wanted the songs as A-sides of 45s but needed B-sides as well. For one of the B-sides, band member Dale Frashuer suggested a song they worked on several years prior called "Kiss Him Goodbye." Leka then decided to include the lyrics "na na na na, na na na na" along with his piano efforts. Mercury really liked the song and wanted to issue it as a single. The musicians involved wanted no part of it and refused to put their names to it. The record company then released it under the group name Steam.

The song came to the attention of a disc jockey (as I've said before, never trust those guys) in Georgia, who decided to play it. At that point, he got a number of requests to hear the song again. When the station put it in their regular playlist, other local stations picked up on the song as well. Apparently, Mercury records heard they were playing it and actually decided to buy one hundred thousand copies of their own record. By doing that, the song would hit the Billboard charts. The move worked, and "Na Na Hey Hey Kiss Him Goodbye" hit number 1 and eventually sold over six million records.

Since that time, a number of sports facilities would play the song when their team won a game or an opposing player was ejected. It has also been played at political rallies for the same reason.

My favorite Steam record
'69: "Na Na Hey Hey Kiss Him Goodbye"

STEELY DAN

Word of caution: This one is not for kids!

Original members
  David Palmer, vocals
  Donald Fagen, lead vocals, keyboards
  Denny Dias, guitar
  Jeff "Skunk" Baxter, steel guitar, percussion (don't want to know how he got that name)
  Walter Becker, bass
  James Hodder, drums

Donald Fagen and Walter Becker put this group together around 1971. Prior to that, they became members of the Don Fagen Jazz Trio, the Bad Rock Group, and the Leather Canary. That group featured an interesting individual on drums by the name of Chevy Chase! (Yes, that Chevy Chase.) For a couple of years, Fagen and Becker were also members of the backup band for Jay and the Americans.

During their years with Jay and the Americans, Fagen and Becker were known as pot-smokin' beatniks. Jay Black (lead singer) suggested the two were the Manson and Starkweather of rock 'n' roll, meaning the infamous Charles Manson and killer Charles Starkweather. (I don't think that was a compliment).

Here's how they came up with the name Steely Dan. Note of caution: You might not want the kids to see this one. It was taken from the book *Naked Lunch* by William Burroughs. It refers to a dildo in the book called *Steely Dan*. (I wouldn't make this stuff up. Well, actually I would, but I didn't have to.)

Steely Dan did have some great success, but much of it was when most of the original members had left the group. Overall, Steely Dan sold more than forty million albums and were inducted into the Rock and Roll Hall of Fame in 2001.

My favorite Steely Dan tunes
'72: "Do It Again"
'73: "Reeling in the Years"
'74: "Rikki Don't Lose that Number"

STRANGELOVES

Original members
  Robert Feldman
  Jerry Goldstein
  Richard Gottehrer

Feldman and Goldstein initially worked together as a duo called Bob and Jerry, followed by (when Gottehrer joined them) Bobbi and the Beaus, Ezra and the Iveys, and the Kittens. None of those groups did anything that actually charted. They were far better known as a songwriting group from Brooklyn, New York. In the early sixties, they became associated with a couple of other groups known as the Angels and the McCoys. They wrote songs for both bands, "My Boyfriend's Back" for the Angels and "Hang on Sloopy" for the McCoys. Both became charted hits.

Then they formed their own group with a strange twist. Even though the group was from New York, they wanted to sound British (Why, why, why? Probably because of the British Invasion), but found they couldn't fake the accent too well. So instead of pretending they were British, they faked that they were Australian. According to their own press material, they were three brothers by the names Giles, Miles, and Niles with the last name Strange. And the Strangeloves were born! They also contended they were Australian sheep farmers! When they performed, they wore vests with zebra stripes and sported African drums. (Okay, Australian with African drums? Those are two separate continents! What were they thinking, or were they?)

Despite the confusion above, the Strangeloves did have a couple of hits, "Hand Jive" and "I Want Candy."

My favorite Strangeloves songs
  '65: "I Want Candy"
  '66: "Hand Jive"

STRAWBERRY ALARM CLOCK

Original members
> Edward King, lead guitar
> Lee Freeman, rhythm guitar, harmonica
> Mark Weitz, keyboards
> Gary Lovetro, bass
> George Bunnell, bass
> Randy Seol, drums

This group was one of the last of the great psychedelic bands of the west coast and formed around 1965. Strawberry Alarm Clock was formed from two other bands of the era, Thee Sixpence and Waterfyrd Traene (sorry, I just don't get those names). The group's success was a number 1 hit called "Incense and Peppermints."

Members of the group say the *strawberry* part of the name was as a tribute to the Beatles song "Strawberry Fields Forever," but they couldn't think of anything to go with it. Finally one of the guys spotted an old alarm clock and said, "How about Strawberry Alarm Clock?" (Well, that makes a lot of sense.) And the rest is history.

My favorite Strawberry Alarm Clock songs
> '67: "Incense and Peppermints"
> '69: "Good Morning Starshine"

STYX

Original members
James Young, vocals, lead guitar
John Curulewski, guitar, keyboards
Tommy Shaw (replaced Curulewski in 1976)
Dennis De Young, keyboards
Charles Panozzo, bass
John Panozzo, drums

This group began in Chicago in 1964 as the Tradewinds. In 1968, they changed their name to the TW4, meaning "then there were four."

In 1972, they were signed to Wooden Nickel Records after an agent became impressed with them at a church concert in Illinois. At this point, they decided to change their name again. Members of the group came up with several suggestions, but according to De Young, the name Styx was "the only one that none of [us] hated," so that was it.

My favorite Styx songs
'72: "The Best Thing"
'74: "Lady"
'75: "Love to Love You Baby"
'76: "Could It Be Magic"

SUGARLOAF

Original members
  Jerry Corbetta, lead vocals, keyboards
  Robert Webber, lead guitar
  Robert Raymond, bass
  Robert MacVitte, drums
  Robert Yezal, guitar
  Robert Pickett, guitar, bass

Looking at the original members this group should have been called Jerry and the Roberts (just my worthless opinion). They actually started as the Moonrakers in 1968 and then became known as Chocolate Hair (that sounds appetizing).

At about that same time, Chocolate Hair signed a recording deal with Liberty Records. Their first song for Liberty, "Green Eyed Lady," became a top 3 hit!

However, before the release of the song, Liberty's legal team got together and became concerned that Chocolate Hair might have some racist overtones for some, so they asked the group to change their name. They decided to take the name of a mountain near Boulder, Colorado (where Bob Webber had a home), and they became Sugarloaf.

My favorite Sugarloaf song
  '70: "Green Eyed Lady"

SUPREMES

Original members
    Florence Ballard
    Mary Wilson
    Diana Ross
    Betty McGlown
    Barbara Martin (replaced McGlown)

These Motowners became the most successful female group in rock history. They had twelve number 1 hits on Billboard. They started as the Primettes in 1959 in Detroit and were the female answer to the male Motown group known as the Primes (soon to become the Temptations). The Supremes even rivaled the Beatles in the midsixties as the most recognizable and popular groups worldwide. What an amazing achievement for a few ladies who originated from the same public housing project in Detroit.

As the Primettes, the group started with Florence Ballard, Mary Wilson, Diana Ross, and Betty McGlown. McGlown left the group in 1960 and was replaced by Barbara Martin. It was at that time they signed with Motown.

As to the origin of their name, that comes from Berry Gordy Jr. He did not approve of the name Primettes. After signing them with Motown Records, he gave the girls a number of names to choose from, including the Darleens, the Melodees, the Royaltones, the Jewelettes, and the Supremes. The group decided on the Supremes even though Diana Ross didn't really like the name; but it stuck. In 1962, Barbara Martin left the group, and the Supremes continued as a trio.

The Supremes had the rare distinction of having four consecutive Billboard number 1 hits, starting with "Stop in the Name of Love," "Back in My Arms Again," "Baby Love," and "Come See about Me."

The Supremes appeared seventeen times on *The Ed Sullivan Show* and have an incredible array of awards. They were inducted into the Rock and Roll Hall of Fame in 1988 and the Vocal Group Hall of Fame in 1998 and received a star on the Hollywood Walk of Fame in 1994. The Supremes and *all* Motown artists are an incredible source of pride for those of us who grew up in Detroit and all of Michigan, including this author.

My favorite Supremes songs
    '64: "Where Did Our Love Go"
    '64: "Baby Love"
    '64: "Come See about Me"
    '65: "Stop in the Name of Love"
    '65: "Back in My Arms Again"
    '65: "I Hear a Symphony"
    '65: "You Can't Hurry Love"
    '65: "You Keep Me Hangin' On"
    '66: "The Happening"
    '66: "Reflections"
    '66: "Love Is Here and Now You're Gone"

TED NUGENT AND THE AMBOY DUKES

Original members
Ted Nugent, lead guitar
Bob Lehnert, vocals
Gary Hicks, vocals, guitar
Dick Treat, vocals, bass
Gail Uptadale, drums

Ted Nugent started performing as early as 1958 when he was ten years old. At twelve, he played with the Royal High Boys and later in 1963 with a group called the Lourds. At that point, he met John Drake, who would later become his lead vocalist with the Amboy Dukes.

Nugent's family moved to Chicago, and there he formed the Amboy Dukes, this time with John Drake as lead singer. Eventually they moved back to Nugent's former hometown of Detroit, Michigan. The group had numerous personnel changes over the years with as many as sixteen different performers.

The name Amboy Dukes came from the title of a novel by American-author Irving Shulman. It was a story about a gang in Brooklyn, New York, during World War II. For a while, Nugent's group called themselves the American Amboy Dukes because they heard there was another group in the UK that went by the same name.

They had one big hit called "Journey to the Center of the Mind."

My favorite Ted Nugent and the Amboy Dukes song
'68: "Journey to the Center of the Mind"

TEMPTATIONS

Original members
    Otis Williams
    Melvin Franklin
    Edward James Kendricks
    Paul Williams
    David Ruffin

The Temps are one of the greatest Motown groups of all time. They repeatedly topped the charts in the sixties and seventies. The group got together in 1960 in Detroit. Members performed with a number of other groups, including the Elgins, Otis Williams & the Distants, and the Primes. During their audition for Motown in 1961, they called themselves the Elgins.

Berry Gordy Jr. agreed to sign the Elgins to a record deal with Motown, but he found out there was another group using the same name. The group then started looking for another name, and according to many, it was Otis Williams, Paul Williams, and songwriter Mickey Stevenson that came up with the name Temptations. The Temptations were known for their great harmonies, their musical style, and their dance moves.

The Temps hit the charts in 1964 with "The Way You Do the Things You Do" and followed that in '65 with their first number 1 hit "My Girl," both written by Smokey Robinson. The group went through a number of personnel and style changes over the years. In 1968, they hit with "Cloud 9," which helped start the psychedelic soul era.

Over the years, the Temptations had four number 1 singles on Billboard's Hot 100 and 14 R & B number 1 hits. They have been credited with three Grammys and a Grammy Lifetime Achievement Award and were inducted into the Rock and Roll Hall of Fame in 1989. They also have three songs in the Rock and Roll Hall of Fame's 500 Songs that Shaped Rock and Roll. They were "My Girl," "Just My Imagination," and "Papa Was a Rollin' Stone."

Interesting note: None of the original members were born in Detroit or Michigan.

My favorite Temptations songs
'64: "The Way You Do the Things You Do"
'65: "My Girl"
'65: "Since I Lost My Baby"
'66: "Get Ready"
'66: "Ain't Too Proud to Beg"
'68: "I Wish That It would Rain"
'70: "Psychedelic Shack"
'70: "Ball of Confusion"
'71: "Just My Imagination"
'72: "Papa Was a Rollin' Stone"
'73: "Hey Girl"

THREE DOG NIGHT

Original members
> Danny Hutton, vocals
> Cory Wells, vocals
> Chuck Negron, vocals
> Jimmy Greenspoon, keyboard
> Joe Schermie, bass
> Michael Allsup, guitar
> Floyd Sneed, drums

Where in the world did that name come from? "Three Dog Night" is one of the most successful rocks bands of the sixties and early seventies. In 1967, vocalists Danny Hutton, Chuck Negron, and Cory Wells first performed together under the name the Redwoods. After adding the four additional members to the group, they took the name Three Dog Night.

There is some dispute as to how the name was selected. The best story (in my opinion) comes from actress June Fairchild, girlfriend of vocalist Danny Hutton. After reading a travel magazine, she mentioned that many Australian Aboriginals were shepherds, and they tended to sleep outside with their sheep and their dogs. On a cool night, they would sleep with one of their dogs to keep warm. The colder it became, the more dogs they would sleep with. Hence, a really cold night was called a Three Dog Night. One of the group's composers, Van Dyke Parks, disputes that story. Parks says that Hutton started a group called Tricycle, which turned into Three Dog Night. Interesting fact is that not one of the members of the group was from Australia.

Without a doubt, though, the first story is much more interesting and entertaining.

Three Dog Night had twenty-one top 40 hits and three number 1 hits in the sixties and seventies. In 1972, they performed on Dick Clark's first *New Year's Eve Show*, and in 2000, they were inducted into the Vocal Group Hall of Fame!

The group still performs to this day (as of 2019).

My favorite Three Dog Night songs
 '69: "One"
 '69: "Easy to Be Hard"
 '69: "Eli's Coming"
 '70: "Celebrate"
 '70: "Mama Told Me Not to Come"
 '71: "Joy to the World"
 '71: "An Old-Fashioned Love Song"

TINY TIM

Herbert Butros Khaury, also known as Herbert Buckingham Khaury, is probably the most successful novelty act the world has ever seen. He performed his unusual act under the names Larry Love, the Human Canary, Derry Dover, and Judas K. Foxglove.

In or around 1965, the name Tiny Tim seemed to fit and stuck for the rest of his career. His biggest break came in 1969 when he appeared on the Johnny Carson show to marry Miss Vicki. It held the biggest audience in television at that time.

Soon after their marriage, Miss Vicki became pregnant. About five months later, their daughter was stillborn. In a bizarre turn, Tim buried the child and had "It" inscribed on the tombstone. (I told you it was bizarre.)

Later, the couple did have another daughter with the name Tulip Victoria. The couple divorced a few years later. Tim died in 1996 of a heart attack.

Tim's biggest hit was the infamous "Tip Toe thru the Tulips."

My favorite Tiny Tim song (sorry Tim or Tiny—only one)
"Tip Toe thru the Tulips"

Although he did have a song called "Tip Toe, to the Gas Pumps," referring to the long gas lines during the OPEC oil crisis in 1973, and "The Hickey on Your Neck," two songs I've never heard but have interesting titles.

TOM JONES

Thomas John Woodward was born in 1940 in South Wales in the UK. He was a choir boy as a child. In his teen years, Woodward put together several singing groups. The first was the Squires, then Tommy Scott & the Senators, and then the Playboys. He also performed as a solo artist as Tiger Tom. During one of his performances in the 1960s in the Playboys, he got the attention of Gordon Mills, a local songwriter, who then took over management of the group. Mills then changed the name of the group to Tommy Scott, the Twisting Vocalist, & His Playboys.

Soon after his stint as the Twisting Vocalist, Woodward moved on to a solo career and took the name Tom Jones to take advantage of the movie of the same name from 1963 (a British adventure comedy). Jones has sold over one hundred million records and has received and incredible number of awards. They include a Grammy, an MTV Video Music Award, two Brit Awards, and an Outstanding Contribution to Music Award. He also did a stint as an actor and received a Golden Globe nomination. In 1999, Queen Elizabeth II knighted Jones for services to music in 2006.

My favorite Tom Jones or "Sir Thomas John Woodward" songs
    '65: "It's Not Unusual"
    '65: "What's New Pussycat"
    '66: "Green Green Grass of Home"
    '67: "Detroit City" (gotta include where I grew up)
    '69: "I'll Never Fall in Love Again"
    '69: "Without Love"
    '71: "She's a Lady"

TOMMY JAMES & THE SHONDELLS

Original members
  Tommy James, vocals, guitar
  Larry Coverdale, lead guitar
  Larry Wright, bass
  Craig Villeneuve, keyboard
  Jim Payne, drums

A great American Pop group from the sixties with roots in Michigan. Tommy James was actually born Tommy Jackson from Niles, Michigan. Tommy formed the band the Echoes in 1959 when he was twelve years old. The Echoes then became Tom and the Tornadoes and released a song called "Long Pony Tail," when all the members were in high school in 1962. In 1964, Tommy renamed the band the Shondells based on a singer he liked, Troy Shondell.

In 1964, Tommy Jackson & the Shondells recorded "Hanky Panky," which did well in Michigan but was not an immediate hit on a national level. At this point, the Shondells decided they were going nowhere and disbanded in 1965 after graduating from high school. (Big mistake!)

In 1965, a promoter found a copy of "Hanky Panky" and started playing it at dance parties in Pennsylvania. Local Pittsburgh radio stations then started playing it, and some unlawful copies were sold in local stores. Tommy James then heard about all this from a Pittsburgh DJ and was asked to bring his group there to hold a concert. Unfortunately, the Shondells were nowhere to be found. James then went alone and found a group called the Raconteurs at a local lounge. He said, "You guys sound pretty good. Would you like to become the Shondells?" They agreed, and they and the song took off.

It was at this point that Tommy Jackson decided to change his name to Tommy James. In 1966, "Hanky Panky" became number 1. They had a number of other hits as well. One of the group's songs had an interesting title inspiration. "Mony Mony" reached number 3 on the Billboard charts, and according to James, the title was inspired by a sign he could see from his room in New York that read "*Mutual of New York.*"

In 1969, James and the group went their separate ways. James went to his new home in New York to recover from a drug problem and then reemerged in 1970 with a successful solo act.

My favorite Tommy James & the Shondells songs
    '66: "Hanky Panky"
    '67: "I Think We're Alone Now"
    '68: "Mony Mony"
    '68: "Crimson and Clover"
    '69: "Sweet Cherry Wine"
    '69: "Crystal Blue Persuasion"

Favorite Tommy James solo song
    '71: "Draggin' the Line"

TURTLES

Original members
    Howard Kaylan, lead vocals
    Mark Volman, vocals
    G. Allan Nichol, lead guitar
    James Ray Tucker, rhythm guitar
    Charles M. Portz, bass
    Donald Ray Murray, drums

This group came out of LA and over the years had over a dozen hits. They started in the early sixties as the Nightriders and later the Crossfires. During that time they became acquainted with local KRLA DJ Reb Foster, who also owned a local club called the Revelaire Club, and he became their manager.

At this point, the group decided they needed a new name. They decided to follow the lead of the Beatles and the Byrds with a critter kind of name that was misspelled. They became the Tyrtles. However, there was probably some mispronunciation of their name, and they reverted to the actual spelling and changed to the Turtles.

My favorite Turtles songs
    '65: "It Ain't Me Babe"
    '67: "Happy Together"
    '67: "She'd Rather Be with Me"
    '68: "Elenore"
    '70: "The Eve of Destruction"

Uriah Heep

Original members
>Mick Box, guitar
David Garrick, vocals
Alex Napier, drums
Paul Newton, bass

Uriah Heep was a group formed in London, England, in the late sixties. In 1967, guitarist Mick Box put together a band in Brentwood, UK, called Hogwash. (Gee, why didn't I come up with a great name like that?) After some personnel changes, they dropped the name Hogwash and came up with the new name Spice. After performing at a number of clubs, they were signed to Vertigo Records.

In 1969, the band decided to change their name to Uriah Heep, based on the villainous character from the book *David Copperfield* (no, not the magician) by Charles Dickens. It was around that time that Dickens's life was being celebrated near the hundredth anniversary of his death.

Their first album, *Very 'Eavy ... Very 'Umble*, did not fare well in the US, though. One writer from *Rolling Stone* said, "If this album makes it, I'll commit suicide." (Well, she did not.)

My favorite Uriah Heep songs
>Sorry, not much of a hard rock and heavy metal fan, but I did love their first name, Hogwash.

Vanilla Fudge

Original members
  Tim Bogert, guitar, bass
  Mark Stein, keyboards
  Vincent Martell, guitar, bass
  Carmine Appice, drums

This group started in New York and played under a number of different names, including Rick Martin & The Showmen, the Electric Pigeons, and then just the Pigeons. They were a rock band that did some heavy rock covers of other hit songs.

According to drummer Carmine Appice, when the group was signed by Atlantic Records, they had some reservations about the name Pigeons. At that point, they played a gig in a Long Island, New York, club, and a girl who worked there told them that her grandfather used to call her Vanilla Fudge. Apparently, she told them the name would work for them because they were a white group that played a lot of soul music. The Pigeons liked it, and Atlantic liked the new name too, so Vanilla Fudge was born.

The group then released "You Keep Me Hanging On" (a rock version of the Supremes' hit) in 1967, but it didn't do much on the charts in the US. It did, however, become a best seller in the UK. The song was then rereleased in America and became a huge hit in 1968.

My favorite Vanilla Fudge song
  '67 and '68: "You Keep Me Hanging On"

Wayne Fontana and the Mindbenders

Wayne Fontana, vocals
Eric Stewart, guitar
Bob Lang, bass
Rick Rothwell, drums

Glyn Ellis was a child star from Manchester, England, who started performing at five years old. At the age of fifteen, Ellis left high school and went into the telephone business. He also formed a singing group called the Jets. He heard about a local club called the Oasis Club that was going to hold an audition by Fontana Records. He tried to convince his group to try out, but only one member, Bob Lang came along. Ellis then talked to a couple of other musicians who were also at the club to join them for the audition.

Surprise, surprise, they were signed by the label. Fontana Records then insisted that Ellis change his name to Wayne Fontana after the label then picked Mindbenders from a movie being featured locally in Manchester. After having a hit song with "Game of Love," Fontana left the group for a solo career. The Mindbenders continued and had a hit with "Groovy Kind of Love."

My favorite Wayne Fontana and the Mindbenders songs
'65: "Game of Love"
'66: "A Groovy Kind of Love" (without Wayne)

Zombies

Original members
   Rod Argent, keyboard and vocals
   Colin Blunstone, vocals
   Paul Atkinson, guitar
   Hugh Grundy, drums
   Chris White, vocals

The Zombies are a British rock group that got together in 1960 in a small town near London called St. Albans. Rod Argent and Colin Blunstone started their endeavor and were joined by Paul Atkinson and Hugh Grundy a year later.

They originally called themselves the Mustangs but soon figured out there were other groups with the same name, so a change was needed. The new name came from Rod Argent, who said he wasn't even sure what *zombies* meant but thought they might be "the walking dead from Haiti." He said he figured it was a name no one else was going to have, so it made sense. Interesting, Arnold left the group not long after the name was agreed on and was replaced by Chris White.

In 1965, they toured the US with great success, and in January of that year, they made their first appearance on American television on the show *Hullabaloo*. They were met with a screaming audience full of teenage girls. (Hmmm, remember it was the Beatles in February of '64 that met the same fate on *The Ed Sullivan Show*.)

In 2012, the Zombies album *Odessey and Oracle* was number 100 on Rolling Stone's Greatest Albums of All Time, and they were inducted into the Rock and Roll Hall of Fame in 2019.

My favorite Zombies songs
   '64: "She's Not There"
   '65: "Tell Her No"
   '69: "Time of the Season"

ABOUT THE AUTHOR

Please allow me to tell you a little about myself. I'm a retired radio personality from the Detroit market. I started my career at a small station, WBRB, in Mt. Clemens, Michigan, in 1978. From there, I moved on to WTWR Tower 92 FM in Detroit, where I did the midday show 10:00 a.m.–3:00 p.m. The format of the station was "Greatest Hits of All Time." We played pop and rock hits from the late '50s through current hits in the late '70s and early '80s. That's where I got my start in oldies music. In 1981, our sister station WCXI needed an FM partner, and our format moved to country music. A few years later, our owner, Gene Autry (that's right, the singing cowboy), sold the stations, and I had to look for something else.

I found out that WHND, Honey Radio, needed an evening host and a promotions director. Happily, I got the job. Honey Radio was all oldies all the time, from the mid-'50s through mid-'70s. This station was very much like stations I grew up with in the '60s. As personalities, we had the opportunity to put listeners on the air and joke with people and just plain have fun.

I nearly got in trouble with the FCC when one evening we were giving away prizes to whomever was the correct caller. In this instance, we gave away what we called a mug and a mug shot. That was a coffee mug with the station's logo and a picture of the DJ giving it away. Well, one of my regular listeners was the correct caller and said, "Oh my god, I've been trying so hard to get this."

I said, "Well, that's nice to hear."

She then said, "I've been wanting a picture of you for so long."

At this point, I was feeling really proud.

Then she said, "I know right where I'm going to hang it."

"Really, and where will you hang it?"

"I'm going to hang it on my bathroom wall."

I said, "Huh."

"That way, if I ever get constipated, it'll scare the shit right out of me."

This was all live on the air. I won't use her last name, but, Beverly, you know who you are! We had a lot of fun at that station, but after several years, the station was leased to a different company, and we lost our jobs.

A few months later, I was hired at WOMC Radio and also played oldies. There I had the opportunity to work as a DJ, news director, public affairs and public service director, and production director.

During my career, I worked with some really great people at all those stations and was going to start naming them, but the list is very long, and there is no doubt I would forget someone, so I will just say, "Thank you, I have a great appreciation for you all."

Along the way, I also had the opportunity to interview dozens of oldies and country performers and got some of the actual stories about their names. I hope this gives you an idea of my experience with oldies pop and rock and roll and why I was intrigued with the idea of writing this book. I retired in 2008 after nearly thirty-one years in the business. I do hope you enjoy.

Please also understand that I make no claim that everything is entirely accurate because there are some conflicting stories from producers and managers and even from some members of the groups in question. Thank you, and again, please enjoy.

Printed in the USA
CPSIA information can be obtained
at www.ICGtesting.com
LVHW091614270924
792308LV00001B/205